MAMA KOKO

and the

HUNDRED GUNMEN

MAMA
KOKO

and the

HUNDRED
GUNMEN

.....

An Ordinary Family's
Extraordinary Tale of Love, Loss,
and Survival in Congo

LISA J. SHANNON

PublicAffairs
New York

Published in the United States by PublicAffairs™,
a Member of the Perseus Books Group

PublicAffairs books are available at special discounts for bulk purchases
in the US by corporations, institutions, and other organizations. For more
information, please contact the Special Markets Department at the Perseus
Books Group, 2300 Chestnut Street, Suite 200, Philadelphia, PA 19103, call
(800) 810-4145, ext. 5000, or e-mail special.markets@perseusbooks.com.

Book Design by Pauline Brown

Library of Congress Cataloging-in-Publication Data

Shannon, Lisa, 1975– author.
  Mama Koko and the hundred gunmen : one ordinary family's
extraordinary tale of love, loss, and survival in Congo / Lisa J. Shannon.
     pages cm
  Includes bibliographical references.
  ISBN 978-1-61039-445-1 (hardcover) — ISBN 978-1-61039-446-8
(e-book) 1. Women and war—Congo (Democratic Republic) 2. War
victims—Congo (Democratic Republic) 3. Atrocities—Congo
(Democratic Republic) 4. Congo (Democratic Republic)—Social
conditions—21st century. 5. Thelin, Francisca. 6. Thelin, Francisca—
Family. 7. Congolese (Democratic Republic)--Biography. 8. Congolese—
United States—Biography. 9. Shannon, Lisa, 1975– —Travel—Congo
(Democratic Republic) 10. Lord's Resistance Army. 11. Kony, Joseph.
I. Title.

  HQ1805.5.S525 2014

  305.9'0695096751—dc23

                                                                  2014035568

  First Edition

                    10 9 8 7 6 5 4 3 2 1

For Heritier

. . . . .

Contents

• • • • •

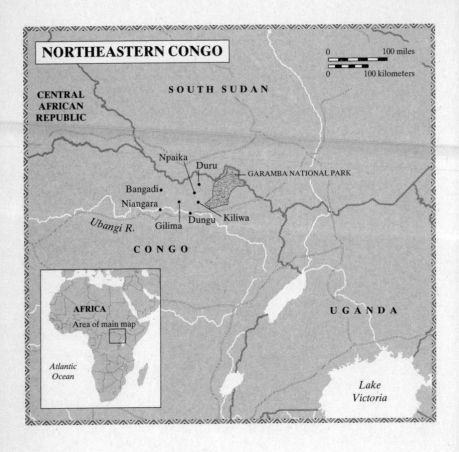

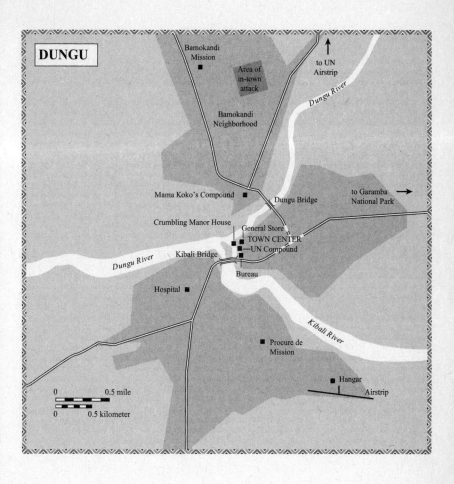

DUNGU

Bamokandi
Mission

Area of
in-town
attack

to UN
Airstrip

Dungu River

Bamokandi
Neighborhood

Mama Koko's Compound

Dungu Bridge

to Garamba
National Park

Crumbling Manor House

General Store
TOWN CENTER
UN Compound

Dungu River

Kibali Bridge

Bureau

Hospital

Kibali River

Procure de
Mission

Hangar

Airstrip

0   0.5 mile

0   0.5 kilometer

MAMA KOKO

and the

HUNDRED GUNMEN

I Imagine

• • • •

Sometimes I imagine standing in the corner of the family coffee plantation, maybe in a nearby field, watching the family hover around Roger's body. The day the attacks started, they found him off the road by the river, in the bushes under a shroud of palm leaves, hacked, his mouth and wounds boiling with a greedy riot of insects.

Roger was the first to die. When the family found his body, neighbors were already rushing to gather their bare essentials, slipping away on the footpaths and back routes, as inconspicuous and silent as a mass exodus can be. Yet Roger's family carried his body back to the coffee plantation for burial.

I picture the family as they linger: mulling around, digging the grave, dressing him for hasty burial. Mama Cecelia kneeling over him, washing away the blood, her calloused fingers sweeping clean every crevasse and axe wound bourgeoning with insects.

Roger's pre-teen sons sulk in the corner, the spark in their eyes draining fast. His church-going wife Marie, tall and full of grace, presses her fingers into a rosary, leaning on Jesus to get

1

her through each imposing minute. Roger's younger brother and another of his sons, each on the verge of manhood, dig the grave. His father Papa Alexander's eyes track the bloodthirsty crawlers shaken free by Mama Cecelia as they make their rapid retreat into dusty fields or dark hiding places, like the neighbors now on their way to Sudan. Maybe he surveys the scene, scanning his coffee kingdom, watching the brush for movement, for clues that scream *Time's up*.

A fatal mistake hangs in the air, between their sighs. The weight of it settles around them, like their hands on each other's shoulders. They do not know that the shreds of human dignity exercised with rituals like washing a beloved's dead body have retreated with the termites into the fields. There would still be time, if the family only knew how to hear Roger's wounds whisper their warning: *You are no longer human. Run.*

Yet they stay, washing their beloved Roger and preparing him for the cold earth. With each swig of tea, each soothing stroke of wet cloth pressing closed Roger's gaping skin, muffling his axe wounds' siren screams, the family exchanges what they do not know will be their final glances between one another.

A Day Like Any Other

• • • •

The same day they buried Roger, on the other side of the world, Roger's cousin Francisca was up at five in the morning, as she was most weekdays, to *put on the pants* as they would have said back home in Congo. It meant *the man goes to work.* Francisca bypassed her stacks of African-print dresses and instead zipped up her slacks right alongside her American husband Kevin, a Peace Corps volunteer turned buttoned-down engineer.

On the way out the door, Francisca caught a glimpse of herself in the mirror: fresh braids bound tight to her head in ornate patterns, shiny dark skin plump with lotion, a dash of ChapStick on her lips, the sum of her makeup routine. Clean and simple, like her mother Mama Koko taught her. *Why cover up all that beautiful?* Francisca greeted herself in the mirror, her coffee-colored eyes rimmed with blue beaming back. As always, she said out loud, "Good morning, lovely!"

Craftsman bungalows pulsed past in the early morning light as Francisca drove to work. She pulled into a mammoth one-stop shopping center, inconceivable back home, compared to her town's one-room general store. Inside cavernous Fred Meyer's, the ambient hum of the ventilation absorbed voices, rattling carts, announcements of spills in aisle nine. Fluorescents washed out the faces of shoppers roaming the windowless open space, packed twelve shelves high with everything from rib-eye steak and bananas on special to cement faeries for the garden, day-to-evening wear, fashion socks, hand blenders, assorted wrenches and paints, fishing gear, and diamond pendants promising to delight and last a lifetime. Everything you need, all in one stop: *You'll Find It at Fred Meyer's.*

Francisca slipped on her chef's coat and pinned on her nametag: "Francisca, Cheese Steward since 1996." Francisca had no background in cheese. There were no sample trays of brie and gruyere, no sharp cheddar finger sandwiches served with iced tea on the old wooden porch of her childhood "castle," as the family called it, overlooking their coffee plantation in that far- northeastern pocket of Congo. Francisca spent her childhood summers roaming in the cotton fields, wading through the cassava leaves, gorging on mangoes and termite-oil delicacies, not cheese.

Francisca didn't even like cheese, though her customers would never know it. She thought of it as *white people's food*. She got the job as cheese steward because she spoke French; French is useful when it comes to cheeses.

That morning, it was out to the floor to organize the olive bar, crowned with gourmet salts from faraway places like the Black Sea and the Himalayas. Anyone browsing the cheese display who listened in would have heard Francisca singing hymns to no one in particular. By the time Francisca finished arranging the display of packaged cuts of cheese in take-home wedges, Roger was already buried on her family's coffee plantation. By then, the family members had split up, and more of them had been murdered by axe.

Francisca was home by noon. She shed her work pants, which reeked of cheese and olive juice, and slipped on one of her African-print skirts. In her living room, surrounded by remnants of home, many-hued dark wood trim blending with ubiquitous African figurines and safari-themed wallpaper, Francisca turned on African music, nice and loud, and danced Congolese style, heavy on the hip thrusts and booty wagging.

Francisca's teenage son Isaac came and went, keeping to himself, as would any proper budding hipster-musician. Francisca didn't like to be alone, and that afternoon she called her Congolese friend Cecile in Wyoming to check in and chat about doctor appointments or the grandkids or to remark on differences in America and Congo—how in America everyone is supposed to *seek counseling* when things get rough. But back home, Francisca just talked to Mama Koko.

One of her grown daughters swung by with the grandkids after school, to say hello and pick something up or drop something off or use the computer or just hang out. Eventually, Francisca got to cooking dinner, very soft beans in the stew and extra peanut butter in the cassava leaves like Mama Koko always did, served with rice—brown rice for Kevin, white for her and the rest of the family.

Then it was early to bed, preparing for another day of *putting on the pants*. As Francisca drifted to sleep that night, she couldn't imagine on the other side of the world Mama Koko lying on an abandoned stretch of road, collapsed from exhaustion, surrounded by wailing grandbabies.

For Francisca, it was a day like any other.

The call came the next day.

It was her friend Cecile, a fellow Congolese-American transplant from Orientale Province. Cecile told Francisca that gunmen—the Lord's Resistance Army (LRA) led by Joseph Kony—had launched massive attacks the previous day in Orientale Province, home to both Dungu, the town where Mama Koko and dozens of Francisca's family members lived, and the village of Duru fifty-some miles north, where Francisca's father had built the family coffee plantation.

Francisca knew of neighboring Uganda's cult militia leader Joseph Kony and his LRA, notorious for abducting more than twenty thousand children and displacing more than 2 million people in Northern Uganda. Kony had formed the LRA in the late 1980s, proclaiming himself a prophet and spirit medium and aiming to base his rule of Uganda on the Bible's Ten Commandments. In 2006, the LRA deserted their Uganda stomping grounds of twenty years and staked out new headquarters next door in Congo. They found ideal conditions to hide under the dense cover of elephant grasses and thick forest canopy of the Garamba National Park, close to the village of Duru, home to Francisca's family coffee plantation. Eventually, the group splintered and spilled into Sudan and the Central African Republic, occupying an area about the size of California. A few dedicated commanders coordinated remotely, often via satellite phone.

Cheap cell phones had recently swept that remote pocket of Congo, so Francisca's family had called before with stories of the LRA stealing from the markets and child soldiers trickling out of the forest hoping to go home. But she'd never heard of attacks on people in Orientale, until that day she got the call from Cecile.

Francisca stayed up all night and into the next day, frantic, camped at her antique dining room table, trying to get through to her family. She would dial, only to get a recording: *The party you are trying to reach is not available*. She'd wait a few minutes, stare at the phone, rest her fingers on the table's protective glass cover. She'd pray to Jesus and Abraham and the ancestors. Then she'd dial again and hear a pick-up, maybe a hello, only to be cut off in two or three seconds. Dial, only to hear the phone ringing and ringing, and no answer. Dial, wondering if she'd ever hear from her family again.

She didn't get through to them that night.

That week, during her days in the cheese department, Francisca told herself *Leave it at the door, professionalism first.* When she failed to corral her thoughts, she ducked before anyone could spot her involuntary tears, and got busy wiping down the countertops, the glass cases, the stainless steel. Some of the other deli-department ladies wanted to know *Why so awfully quiet? How come her eyes are so red?* She didn't mention the late-night crying spells sopping her pillows. "I'm just tired. Didn't sleep so well."

Her granddaughters tried to air out her mood, but when she heard them whisper *Uh, oh, she's crying again,* Francisca decided it was unfair to weigh down the family. She did her best to keep updates brief, daily routines in motion, and dinners cheery. Luckily, Kevin was an early and heavy sleeper. Still, her sons peppered her with *Are-you-okays,* despite her reassurances she was fine.

One of her sons, Solomon, said, "Your eyes are red."

"I'm tired."

He urged her to try to set it aside. "Can't you just let it go?"

After Kevin and the kids went to bed, she stayed up, every night, most nights until after one in the morning, hoping to reach someone, anyone, who might know if Mama Koko was okay, if the family was still alive. She took short breaks to pray in front of the guest-room shrine, a wall packed with Catholic religious icons mixed with photos of her beloved departed. Then back to the dining room table for endless touch-tone dialing.

Finally, one night, a cousin answered the phone. Francisca blurted out her one and only question: "Is everyone okay?"

Then she heard gunshots, and the line went dead.

The Year of Bad News

• • • •

Out of our puttering five-seater charter plane, Francisca and I looked down eight thousand or so feet to Congo below. Above the land leading to Dungu, vast blankets of the Congo basin forest stretched to the horizon in all directions, rivers slicing through, catching the sunlight. The canopy was too thick to see through, leaving what was beneath entirely to the imagination, aside from a couple of mining towns and tiny settlements on remote bends in the river.

It had been a year of bad news since the day Francisca got that first call. She was tired, distracted, spending almost every night up, trying to get through to her family for news, unhinged by the media reports intermittently firing across the international wires, mixed with static-marred cell phone calls from home. Sometimes she could talk for a minute or two before the line cut out. Sometimes, in the middle of the night, after she had finally gotten to sleep, her phone would ring and, panicked, she'd jump out of bed and run to answer it, her hands shaking so much that she fumbled when she tried to pick up, hitting the wrong buttons.

Occasionally, Francisca's calls made it through to her brothers or Mama Koko, when they weren't spending months at a time hiding in the bush. No one had died the day she heard gunshots and the line went dead, but that was little consolation. Every call yielded broken, hasty reports of gunmen and cousins, nieces, nephews, and more cousins killed, abducted, burned alive on Christmas Day.

I found myself at Francisca's dining room table that fall into spring into summer and back into fall, not because I was her close friend but because her family was smack-dab in the middle of Congo's latest firestorm. I'd known Francisca since 2005, three years earlier, when my do-or-die Congo activism began.

I didn't know much about Congo before 2005. I'd read half of Joseph Conrad's *Heart of Darkness* in college, before dropping my "Literature of Colonialism" class. I might have seen something about militias and massacres in Congo on an episode of *ER*, but figured it was fictionalized for the show's melodramatic effect. Eventually, it was an episode of *The Oprah Winfrey Show* that hooked me. The catalytic episode was a documentary-style report about both the war raging in Congo's far-eastern provinces—where millions had died in the deadliest war since World War II—and the rape crisis there, which had metastasized into a pandemic, the worst on earth. But the war and rape pandemic were virtually ignored by the US media and by policy makers around the world. The camera lingered on the eyes of the Congolese women as they told their stories. It stirred something in me. A metamorphosis began.

That first year, I created Run for Congo Women, a fundraiser for Women for Women International's sponsorship program. I—the wimpy runner—did a thirty-mile trail run, alone. The $28,000 I raised went straight to women in Congo. The next year, I set a goal of a million dollars, hoping to start a movement for Congo. I edited my life, swapping my photography business's cash-flow charts and sales reports for dusty trail runs and sweltering advocacy days in DC. I traded out my fiancé (he wasn't up to the shift in direction) for my new Congolese sisters. Every square inch of my life was dedicated to my work for Congo.

In 2005, that first year, a former missionary to Congo had struck up a conversation with Francisca at the cheese counter, and invited us both over for tea and Congo talk.

Back then, Francisca glowed when she talked about home, sharing meticulously organized albums containing photos of her family sitting in front of lush flower gardens, posing with fish the size of children, standing next to the town's colonial manor house, vegetation sprouting from every window and eave in its slow-motion tumble into the Kibali River.

It was through these photos that Francisca first introduced me to her family, the cousins and nieces and nephews and uncles, before so many of the pictured were killed, before Francisca ever thought all those deaths even possible. I saw her father André on his coffee plantation, a broad smile spread across his face, the ease of a man comfortable in his skin. André's only brother Alexander looked well groomed, with the knowing sideways smile of a younger brother who had come into his own.

And then there was Mama Koko, a name meaning *great-grandmother* in their native tongue of Lingala. I'd never seen a great-grandmother look so good. In one photo, adult Francisca posed playfully on Mama Koko's lap, both laughing. They look like sisters, an impression buoyed by their twinsy outfits. Each of their wardrobes was composed mostly of swaps or duplicates. Whenever Francisca found a beautiful Dutch Super Wax fabric, she bought enough for two dresses and sent the balance back home to Mama Koko. Sometimes she and Mama Koko made nearly identical dresses with the matching fabric—piping, buttons up the front, oversized caps sleeves for drama—even though they didn't plan it that way and the cloth was tailored on different continents.

Francisca urged me to join her there someday, for a slice of the real Congo, peaceful Congo.

I wasn't interested. My focus was on Congo's war.

But during that year of bad news, we sat together at her dining room table over many a cup of peach tea, both of us suspended somewhere between Congo and America.

Then it dawned on me: What if we could go to Dungu together, just as she had suggested so many times before? Even if the US media weren't covering Kony's attacks on her homeland, her remote pocket of Congo, *we* could collect her family's stories and share them with the world. Maybe Francisca could transform those anxious nights into a greater good. Maybe I could help her help her people.

We were wading into a deeper crocodile swamp than we knew, of course. We couldn't see then what our prodding might unravel. Or the fact that by the time our story reached its end, so many of the people central to our time in Dungu would be dead.

At the time we dreamed up our journey, it seemed purely good.

Francisca mulled over the notion of a joint trip to Dungu. All those losses. All those late nights. All those groggy mornings, up early to peddle gourmet salts to aspiring foodies who would never ask or understand her newly tired eyes.

Francisca decided to go.

Dust

• • • •

Our plane skipped along a dirt landing strip stamped into a grassy field on the edge of Dungu. Francisca's family members, about twenty of them, emerged from the shadows of the brick hangar and stood at attention as our plane came to a stop. To Francisca, after endless ringing and ringing and what-might-have-happened redials, it felt surreal. Looking out the tiny window at her beloved familiars, they now seemed somehow unfamiliar. This was not the joyous celebration of previous arrivals: Francisca could see by the way they held themselves that things had changed. The mournful drape of skinnier bodies, panicked eyes, the roomy smiles that had once greeted her now collapsed. They all looked older.

Dungu smacked of dust and heat. It hadn't rained yet that season, a misfortune worn by every blade of roadside grass, hovering in the air, sucked in with each gritty breath. Wisps of ash swarmed in drifts against a dull sky.

I followed as Francisca stepped down from the plane, enveloped by family under the wing. She embraced Mama Koko first. They both cried with relief.

As family members took their turns to say hello to Francisca, each holding on extra long and hard, Mama Koko stood back.

She wore a vivid print dress and wrap like the rest of the women, each bursting with colors and patterns. Unlike the others who clutched their handbags and donned Sunday-best wigs and heels, Mama Koko wore comfortable sandals and a loose wrap. Her hair was cut close to her head for low maintenance. She held herself with an easy grace that must come with being the family's presiding matriarch.

Gunshots echoed across town, from the direction of Mama Koko's place. Francisca watched the family exchange tense glances. Francisca looked over at me, snapping photos, oblivious. She wondered: *Should I tell her?*

We'd almost canceled the trip. About a week before our departure, Francisca got another bad-news call about a fresh attack.

Most attacks raged in the countryside north of Dungu, driving villagers into town, under the shadow of the United Nations compound and the Congolese army patrols. But a week before our trip, an attack happened *inside* Dungu. As if calling a bluff, the gunmen just strolled into town. Right past the UN airstrip. Right past Congolese army patrols. The LRA opened fire on residents, killing, abducting, beating a woman to death with firewood.

No one—not the United Nations, not the Congolese army—intervened.

It happened about a mile from Mama Koko's home, where we had been planning to stay.

Before Francisca got the news, Kevin and their kids hadn't offered any commentary on our plan. Francisca could feel it, though: They didn't want her to go. When Francisca mentioned the in-town attack to Kevin, he didn't say much, but Francisca's daughter Lomingo came over and gave her a talking-to about abandoning the trip. "But think how you would feel if it was me over there," Francisca said. "If I don't go now, I may never see Mama Koko again."

Francisca knew she had to tell me about that attack. When she called, I could hear the angst in her voice—fear, but not for her own safety, or mine. She was scared that I would cancel. And she wouldn't go alone.

I said, as though willing it to be true, "We'll be fine."

"We'll be fine," Francisca said.

"We'll be fine."

"Yeah. We'll be fine."

Neither of us slept that night. When we talked the next day, we stumbled on an eerie kismet: We'd both dreamed the night before that the LRA cut off our arms.

At the time, I tried to problem-solve. I sought counsel from policy experts. Some advised that the key was having a getaway vehicle and staying on the other side of town. I asked my friend Sasha, who had spent two years in Northern Uganda, "So, if we see the LRA, any safety tips?"

Stunned by the naiveté of the question, he replied, "If you see the LRA, *you're dead.*"

LRA gunmen were spotted in Mama Koko's neighborhood the morning of our arrival.

Francisca was plenty safety-conscious. She was so nervous about the rape crisis to the south that she wore layers of tights and leggings under her skirt throughout our layover in Ituri. She figured the layers would slow any would-be predator while she screamed for help. But when she heard the gunshots on the landing strip, she decided we were already in Dungu. There was nothing to be accomplished by freaking out her American travel companion with reports of gunfire.

Francisca decided to keep it to herself.

Dette

• • • •

Francisca introduced me to Mama Koko, who seemed almost shy as she smiled and nodded formally while we shook hands. But with no words in common, the undercurrents of this kind of vague pleasantry are so often misunderstood. She was sizing me up, just as she had Kevin so many years ago.

As though Mama Koko understood English, I said, "So lovely to finally meet you. I've heard so much about you!"

We slid onto the peeling vinyl seats of a banged-up Toyota 4Runner that would transport us across town. I turned to look at Mama Koko and Francisca in the back seat. When Francisca showed me her family photo albums back in Portland, Oregon, I thought that Mama Koko and Francisca looked the same age, despite their sixteen-year difference. But crammed against these peeling vinyl seats, Mama Koko looked like the younger of the two, next to Francisca's graying hair. Mama Koko carried herself with the reserve and grace of a woman who'd been worshiped by men for a lifetime. Back when she was young Bernadette, her long hair and gap-toothed smile made her the definition of beauty in these parts.

She was born around 1940, to mother Vivica (later known as Tita Vica) and father Bi. Her father was the first child of Bondo and Nahilite. He was a twin, hence the name Bi. In Dungu, twins are always named Bi—first twin—and Siro—second twin. Girl or boy, it doesn't matter. The issue for Bondo and Nahilite was that after the boy twins, they had a set of girl twins. They dutifully named the girls Bi and Siro, like their brothers. Even with Nahilite's third pregnancy, and the subsequent birth of yet another set of girl twins, they followed the custom and named the girls Bi and Siro. The fourth set of twins, this time a boy and a girl, was another story. To avoid confusion, they broke with the custom and named the babies Fabino and Veronique. Shortly thereafter, when Nahilite was pregnant with what everyone assumed was a fifth set of twins, she died due to complications with the pregnancy. All of the other twins lived to adulthood.

Mama Koko, young Bernadette, was married as an infant, though she didn't know it until she was called out of class at the age of twelve. Her classmates and the nuns watched as the young beauty in her Catholic-school uniform arrived in the mission's courtyard garden to find a strange old man waiting for her, introducing himself as her husband.

She mostly noticed he was *old*. As in way older than a twelve-year-old. As in who cares what he was wearing, where he worked, if he had money, why he was there . . . *old*. He hovered and declared he had come to claim her. She wept, protesting until the priest called her into his office, along with the old man and her father Bi, who, it turned out, had made the arrangement at Bernadette's birth.

The custom dictated that when a woman was pregnant, any want-to-be husband planted a special flower in front of her home. If the baby was a girl, and the parents kept the flower, it meant their daughter was betrothed. Apparently Bi and Vivica let this man's flower stay on. One can't say why motherless Bi would care to marry off his infant daughter, or why his word was strictly adhered to, but Bi was a man who stuck to his commitments.

Nonetheless, the priest asked Bernadette, "Do you want to marry this man?"

"No."

"Then it's decided," the priest decreed.

Bi did not speak to his daughter for three years. Nor did Bernadette speak to her father. Silence hung in the family home like a death sentence. The priest had issued her the one and only intervention she would ever get. With each new suitor, the threat was sharpened: Get married or die, if not by a rejected would-be husband, then dad would do the job.

Bernadette focused on squeezing every last drop out of school before that dreaded event.

At fifteen, Bernadette finished the fifth grade, which the Belgians—during their colonization of Congo—deemed the highest level of education necessary for the Congolese. Few went on to sixth grade or beyond. It didn't matter how smart or dedicated a student Bernadette may have been.

When the school year ended, Bernadette retreated to the family farm to help her mom, as she did every July. One day, they told her to dress up and get out to the receiving room.

A man had come calling. André worked at the general store. He had spotted Bernadette in town running errands with her mother.

André and his only brother Alexander were both sons of Gamé, who had four wives and forty-three children. André was more like a father to Alexander, who was more than twenty years his junior and the youngest of the forty-three children. They had grown up on their father's land in then–Belgian Congo, picking cotton for the Belgians and Greeks who had come to the colony to build their personal empires.

For the most part André and Alexander didn't mind the white people. Except, of course, if André or Alexander or any of the other workers got behind in planting and the white people made them lie on the ground and whipped them like they were slaves. If anyone did *anything* they deemed bad, like brew local liquor, they beat the offender. As Alexander would later recall, "They had a right to do it because they were white. They acted like they owned people."

André did not intend to spend his life picking cotton. He got a job as a salesman for the local Greek shopkeeper who ran the general store in town so he could observe, up close, how to run a business. That's where he spotted Bernadette.

Peeking out into the private family receiving room, Bernadette knew the game was up. Bi had entertained other suitors outside like any other visitor, but he invited this man into the private family home. He was serious.

André was about thirty years old and his salesman job was respectable, on a par with Bi's work as a watchman for the cotton company. Bernadette knew that her parents would never push for her to go back to school.

The way she figured it, she had two choices: Marry this man, or escape.

She accepted the proposal and stalled. André visited often, and took to calling her *Dette* for short. She laughed and charmed and played along. All the while, she was scheming that when the time was right she would make a run for it, far away, to a life entirely her own.

After months of long talks together, André came to escort Dette to his home. Her mother and aunt gathered her things and walked with her on the mile-long trek into the center of town, where André lived in a couple of rooms attached to the back of the store. They left her with a pile of wedding gifts, mostly household items like baskets and spoons and cooking pans that she didn't know how to use. Dette had been too focused on math tables and calligraphy to learn the domestic arts. Doing laundry, scouring scalded pots, following a good recipe for leafy greens— none of these had ever entered her daily routine, a major flaw in her fake-wife charade.

But the biggest threat to Dette's grand getaway scheme turned out to be André himself. Instead of beating her or mocking her lack of domestic prowess, for a month André patiently taught Dette. They did laundry together. They scoured pots, swept, husked rice, and cooked leafy greens. They fed and clothed André's young brother, eleven-year-old Alexander, who decided that Dette was his new mother, even though she was only four years his elder.

No, André didn't pounce on her. But sometime during that month of new marriage, sometime between the cooking lessons, the shared rice and burnt fish, the shopping trips to the market, maybe in the dark hours in their dark room behind the store, hands wandered. For a few minutes, the gap-toothed, long-haired beauty abandoned her getaway plan.

Dette buried her dream of escape forever in the quiet moment she realized she was pregnant with their first baby, Francisca.

Lost Shiny

· · · ·

On shock absorbers worn to nothing, the 4Runner—or "Runner," as I called it—bounced and lurched along the open fields on the outskirts of town. Cattle grazed with white crane-like birds perched on their backs. "Beya," Francisca said. When she was a child, the kids all chanted and clapped a little song to those birds: *Beya pesa ngai pembe, napesa yo moindo. If you give me your whiteness, I will give you my blackness.*

The children would point out little pale spots on their skin, like under their fingernails, and declare, "See! I'm turning white!" Years later, the joke took hold with Kevin. They would point at her pale nail beds or his freckles. *See, I'm turning white! See, I'm turning black!*

Smoke rose from the blackened ground along the edge of the road like smoldering arteries as huts grew denser, hedges or twig-fences defining the yards—"parcels," as locals called them. Each parcel consisted of several round adobe huts, topped with straw and supported with crooked, polished wooden poles. Wood and woven palm-leaf chairs followed the shade across each yard. Locals were burning away the roadside brush for easier LRA sightings.

Dungu's soil was hard-packed under the weight of the 100,000 extra heads lying down for the night, the extra 200,000 feet pacing its grounds. We couldn't see them from the main road, but tucked away under shady palm groves and fields designated for planting, the town bulged with refugees living in tents made of palm leaves, open fire pits out front, next to oil cans marked *USA: Not for Resale*. Dungu was comfortably suited to fit its 25,000 residents. By January 2010, it had swollen—according to reports from Francisca's family—to 125,000, due to an influx of those fleeing surrounding villages in LRA territory.

On our flight's descent, we could see the town radiating from converging rivers—the Dungu and the Kibali. The south was the safer part of town: the airport, the hospital, the big mission, the *Procure de Mission* where we arranged to stay after news of the in-town attack. The main road ran through the center of town and then arched across the Dungu River, splitting into two roads stretching upward, like arms flung open in celebration, or hands cradled in offering. That neighborhood to the north, that offering, was Bamokandi, the site of the most recent attack. Mama Koko's place sat on that junction. With the exception of the UN airbase, everything, even one mile beyond Bamokandi, was considered LRA territory.

As we approached the town center, it was obvious that the Belgians had had some kind of grand plan for this place. Who wouldn't? Open grassy fields on the banks of converging rivers must have positively screamed for a manor house. And they got one.

The story went that back when Congo was still a colony Belgium funded a two-lane bridge across the Kibali, but the Belgian administrator responsible for the project built just the one lane to specifications, with its frills and high arches. He used the remaining funds to build himself a European manor house on the Kibali's banks, like a welcome gate. The house was abandoned at Independence. By the 1970s, its roof had caved in, but the floors still held strong. Locals used it for terrace parties for a time; Francisca and Kevin attended dances there in the 1980s. By 2010, the manor was a roofless mass of plants and stone crumbling into the river: Townspeople, chickens, bicyclists with precariously balanced loads, and SUVs still shoved past each other between the brittle archways of its half bridge. The single slender lane stretching across the Kibali River was the only passage from the south into the center of town.

We bounced across the river in our Runner. I watched the water gliding over smooth rocks below, reeds and grasses bent with the breeze, so inviting. It made me thirsty. It made me want to rip off the suffocating black cotton sticking to my limbs. "It makes me want to swim."

"Not safe," Francisca said. "Crocodiles."

Among the polished rocks, women laid out laundry to dry as water rushed through the rusted skeleton of a truck. According to Francisca, the driver had plowed straight off the bridge, made the long drop, and crashed the truck. He walked away from the accident without much more than a few scratches. A few months later, when he was hunting in the bush, a buffalo killed him. When I remarked on the irony, Francisca shrugged. "When it's your time, it's your time."

Downtown Dungu was a ghost of someone's colonial dream. Long rows of ancient mango trees lined the main roads, reminiscent of the driveways to southern plantations. Everything was scattered wide, in overgrown fields that never became the thriving town center: a government office here, a police station there, in the shade of a mango tree. Mostly the buildings, stamped with old bureau or shop names, were empty cement shells, or boarded up, in various states of decay. Some had rotten doors swung open to building innards that now housed only piles of broken bricks fixed in place by fast-growing weeds.

An old-fashioned general store, labeled with Greek lettering from the colonial days, marked the center of town. Its cracked front steps led up to a wide, wraparound veranda. Inside, the old Victorian-era wooden shelves held the best of Dungu's imported goods.

We needed water, so Francisca's brother Antoine ran inside while we stalled outside the store. I looked back at the cathedral of ancient mango trees hovering over brick walls capped with razors: the United Nations compound. From the road, we could see just the tops of their sterile-white cargo containers serving as offices and housing. That compound was where whites used to play tennis when Francisca was a child, and where Kevin played hackie-sack in the '80s.

I stared down Dungu's other main street, about two blocks long, a row of old shops with wide columns and frilly Victorian embellishments ornamenting the porches, broken or in half-hearted states of repair. Most of the shops looked closed. A couple of hopeful stalls were set up on the road, at the base of mango trees. Each had a simple plank. One belonged to a local artist who sold decorative ebony carvings; the other held about a dozen reused bottles of petrol.

Those were my impressions of Dungu, ten minutes deep.

To Francisca, Dungu was something else entirely. She noted what had changed since her last visit. "In Dungu, we have dark skin and we're shiny. People lost their shiny."

"From malnutrition?" I asked.

"From misery."

"We slept there," Mama Koko said from the backseat of the Toyota 4Runner, gesturing toward one of the covered verandas, referring to the family's quasi-refuge during attacks, when they camped out in front of the UN. She had a straightforward, just-the-facts manner. No recounting of *the horror, the horror*. She pointed to the opposite veranda: "There, too."

Francisca skimmed the scene with its familiar textures of home. Her first memories faded in at that very spot, under the Greek lettering, in the Dungu general store.

Harvest

• • • •

Francisca first remembers looking at general-store customers through glass display cases, listening to the rattle of sewing machines making ladies' dresses on the spot, the songs of women camped on the front porch cleaning coffee beans and little fish, their harmonies echoing into the shop. Her dad André was still a salesman at the general store, working for the Greek owner. He took her to work, where she sat behind the counter, surrounded by dry goods stacked on shelves so high it seemed like the tops disappeared into the shadows of the ceiling. Customers were greeted on their way in by displays of ladies' cloth, piles of beans along one side, bags of dried sardines and big cuts of smoked fish along the other.

Francisca, or *Cisca* as they called her then, didn't know much about white people—just the Greek store owner and those she met when her dad took her out to eat at the *Bon Garcon*, the Good Boy, where she gorged on bread. Sometimes little Cisca got bored with the grown-ups coming and going at the store, so she slipped out back to play with the Greek's son Nico, who was about her age. They spent hours playing with his toys from Europe, wind-up cars and wooden choo-choo trains.

Kids in Dungu didn't have toys like that. Mama Koko—*Dette* back then—taught little Cisca how to make baby dolls out of husks from banana trunks. Sometimes she sawed off the ends of corncobs and arranged them upright like bowling pins so Cisca and her brothers could bowl them down with oranges.

One day Nico's dad sent a gift for little Cisca: a toy horse-scooter, one whose head bobbed up and down as the children scooted it around the yard. Nico's dad had brought it all the way from Greece. Cisca and her brothers squealed with delight as they rode their new metal horsey, head bobbing as they crisscrossed their own dirt tracks. Little Cisca was so enthralled by the new toy that it took a while for her to notice the cars speeding by.

When she finally looked up, she saw all the white people's cars on their way out of town, their roofs piled high with everything they owned roped down, covered in tarps.

She asked her mama Dette, "What's going on?"

"We got independence," Dette answered. "The white people have to leave."

Little Cisca would later learn that "We got independence" meant that the Belgians had finally released their colonial claim on Congo and granted sovereignty. Congolese collective resentment over decades of maiming, murder, and rubber shipped downriver sent most white people fleeing for fear of reprisals.

"What about Nico?" Cisca asked. She set aside her horsey and watched the road, hoping to see her playmate. His parents' little car did eventually speed by, piled with stuff just like the others. Francisca waved, hoping to say good-bye. The whole family joined her in waving. The Greeks didn't wave back. She figured they were probably going too fast to even see her.

The Greek owner gifted his employees with the goods he had to leave behind. In André's years working at the general store, he'd studiously observed the Greeks doing business. André and Dette lived on a prime piece of real estate, right on Dungu's junction to the north. Men began delivering cases of beer to the house, and André and Dette set up a shop all their own.

André noted that all the Greeks and Belgians had farms on the other side of the river, growing their own coffee and cotton. On the road a few miles outside of the village of Duru, André spotted a beautiful piece of dense jungle. No one lived out that far, but the trees with big thorns grew there. He knew that meant rich soil, perfect for a plantation. He approached the village chief about a purchase.

Dette managed the store in Dungu, while André and Alexander cleared three acres of jungle and hired a few families to help plant his first crop of coffee, cassava, rice, and peanuts.

Dette and André wasted nothing. Their plantation and shop ran on order, while home and family ran on Dette's passion for clean. Even at the start of their new life, André's clothes were pressed every day; Dette's hair was always in fresh braids. The children bathed every day, the girls twice. Francisca didn't wear clothes like the other girls did, store-bought dresses or imported used clothes from the markets, which they called *tombola bwaka*—Lingala for "lift and throws" or, in Zande, *zili bwana*, "rotten person's clothes." Instead, Dette made dresses for Cisca from scratch. She made them fancy, with polka dots, elastic waists, puffy sleeves, buttons up front, oversized pockets, and full skirts to twirl in the wind.

In the late afternoons, Dette braided Cisca's hair, while Cisca napped, draped over Dette's knees. The day ended with a lotion rubdown, and not the store-bought kind. Dette's mother Vivica, who they called Tita Vica ("Grandmother Vica"), whipped together batches of homemade lotion consisting of palm nuts, lemon, and honey.

Tita Vica was still young and strong then, beautiful in her fancy wax dresses. Francisca tagged along with Tita Vica to the Dungu River to collect baskets full of fish in homemade traps. Tita Vica kept a special little chair for Francisca at her hut, where no one else was allowed to sit. She washed Francisca's feet, propped them up, and served her treats, like fresh-squeezed mango juice.

On the plantation, there was a time for everything. Coffee came in the fall. By Christmas they had rice and millet. Termites came in the springtime. Dette collected, boiled, and dried them, then wrapped them in a cloth, slowly squeezing out the termite oil, a delicacy for the year. Fruit ripened during summer vacation—lemons, avocado, guava, papaya, mango.

When André's first harvest came in, they collected a full ton of rice, plus stacks of coffee. It was enough to reinvest and grow the plantation out to the stream running on the land's perimeter.

Francisca's summer break coincided with the peanut harvest every July. As soon as school was out, Dette and André loaded the kids up on their bikes and rode out to Duru. They could make it in one day if the smaller kids didn't fidget and ask for too many pee breaks.

Monkeys dangled around in the forest surrounding the field, eyeing the crops, watching as Dette corralled the children out to the fields. The children sang all day as they and Dette and André worked alongside the farm hands pulling up the peanuts.

Francisca and her parents planted a small tree in their yard, as was the custom, and drew a circle around it with ash. Every morning, at the feet of this tree, her dad said a prayer to the spirits and placed an egg in its branches. They raised their heads, drank water, and thanked the spirits who brought food and protected the family.

When the rains didn't come, they woke very early and went to the nearby creek with a white chicken, feet bound, along with her eggs and a bundle of rice. Spirits of the forest and ancestors lived around streams, and everyone knew if you wanted to reach them, night was the time. They dumped all the food and the chicken, bound, into the river. The chicken sank to the bottom and drowned, as the family prayed for rain.

Soon enough, André had six people working on his farm and he built a wooden house for the family to live in during their school vacations: a rectangular house of all wood with two bedrooms, and a living room with chairs made of bamboo. The three steps up to the front door made it a grand place, one they nicknamed "the castle."

This might have been the time a successful son of a polygamist, one of forty-three children belonging to four mamas, would think about a second, or third, or fourth wife. André didn't. "Too much drama," Mama Koko said decades later. She added, "I wouldn't have cared if he did. I always knew I was the one."

André was crazy for Mama Koko. He would burst into song in front of the whole family: *Oooh, my wife Dette! Oooh my wife Dette!*

It made her uncomfortable. "Oh, would you stop."

Still, he'd go on about her during meals. "Wow! My wife really knows how to cook!"

"Calm down and eat," she'd say. "You don't have to preach about it."

After dinner, André would get the kids to sing: church songs, new songs, any songs. He closed his eyes and waved his hands in the air in tempo. Dette would offer dryly, "See, kids, the angels are turning around your dad."

As Cisca got older, she offered to do all the other chores, like cleaning, boiling the water, making dinner—anything other than pulling the peanuts. She gave the farm workers' children hard candies from the general store as a preemptive thank-you for their help with her duties. André was not impressed. "You better hold tight to your pen, girl! You're not cut out for life on some farm. Study. Maybe you'll marry a white guy and you can eat bread!"

For many families there was nothing extra for a harvest celebration, but Cisca's family hosted one almost every year, a feast to thank the spirits. They timed it so the full moon could light the place up. No need to decorate. The fruit trees surrounding their home were decoration enough. Cisca knew the feast was coming when Dette began to prepare the millet wine, cooking it slowly, slowly in water, over a fire. Then she smoked fish, dried gourds for cups, made a special banana drink for the kids.

By Saturday afternoon, neighbors began to show up, with chairs and drums carved out of wood, strapped down with goat skins. The millet wine flowed, drums started thump-thump-thumping, and singing and dancing commenced. Everyone danced in a circle around the drummers: grandmas, kids, neighbors, André getting down. Dette didn't usually dance, but at the harvest feast she full-on shook it.

Cisca and her brothers and sisters ate everything, including wild black and white birds collected from the forest, cooked in termite-oil sauce. To little Cisca, it was no-tomorrow yummy. As the evening slid into night, the kids were stuffed with treats and sent to bed. But they stayed awake, listening to the dancing and singing, creeping out to spy as the party thumped on until the sun came up.

Cisca fell asleep thinking: *I am like a princess.*

Still Nursing

• • • •

We pulled up to Mama Koko's place, a one-story road-front cement house, dripping with bright orange climbers. It stood just one block from the Dungu Bridge, the gateway to the Bamokandi neighborhood, which was the site of the in-town attack and LRA sighting earlier that day.

André and Bernadette had bought the land more than half a century before, but long gone were the shelves of household goods and cases of beer. The land was now only half hers, and not by choice. It sat right on the main junction, next to a roundabout crowned with a statue of a native warrior, marking the fork in two roads heading north. Because of the house's strategic position on the road and its strong cement walls, the Congolese army kicked the family out when it suited them, and of late, that was often. The family had moved back in only four days before our arrival.

We slipped inside the three-bedroom house, where extended-family members squished together politely in the living room, watching Francisca, Mama Koko, and me feast on an astounding by-request vegan meal: pumpkin-seed dumplings, fried bananas, homemade soy milk, brown rice with cooked cassava leaves known as *pondu*, bean stew, and sweet pineapple.

But it was a welcome feast among ruins. Devastation hung in the air, like the gunshots everyone heard earlier that day. The children crowded around us, watching keenly as we ate the elaborate spread, mamas chastising them to stand back. The children ate only one meal a day, and this wasn't it.

Everything had changed. All of the treasured household items were stolen when the Congolese army took over. Mama Koko stashed their remaining good dishes and furniture with friends on the other side of town. She didn't replace them. She didn't keep anything nice anymore. She knew they would be taken, again.

After we ate, we resettled into the backyard *yapu*, a large open-air hut made of palm leaves and adobe, furnished with traditional woven lounge chairs and wooden coffee tables. This was the real living room on the property, where kids played, women cooked, and guests were welcomed.

André's grave sat off to the side, with a couple of other family tombs, large coffin-shaped cement blocks graced with rainbow pinwheels and the wires of decapitated plastic flowers cemented into cans in place of a headstone. Francisca had brought these love-gifts from America to honor the family members who died when she was so far away, but the plastic flowers had long ago been lifted by grave robbers. Only the rainbow pinwheels remained, spinning cheerfully in the breeze.

The rest of the sprawling property, well over an acre in size, was dotted with traditional adobe huts for family and squatters. Mama Koko lived in the back in a traditional hut, not in the cement house.

In the *yapu*, family gathered in a loose circle and small talk lurched along—how big the children had grown, the new babies born—and soon Mama Koko and the rest were hungry to share, their minds and tongues fixed on the in-town massacre only days before. Francisca stalled, asking after neighbors and old friends.

She had always avoided blood and gore: When she was a kid, she wouldn't kill a goat or hen like her brothers and sisters did. Back in Portland, Kevin always came home from the video store with *his* and *hers* movies: an action flick for himself and a smooth comedy for Francisca. While he watched his shoot-ups, she roamed the house in self-imposed exile. She couldn't look at that stuff. She knew they were only movies, but she cried every time someone was killed.

That first afternoon in Dungu, the family wanted to talk. Some sat close to Francisca and held her hand. Francisca wasn't ready. She didn't want to know the details yet, what had been stolen, what they'd never get back, as if putting off the full report could make it less real. She wanted home to still be home.

It was easier for her to steer the conversation toward me, the guest. In the United States, we often lead with the question *What do you do?* In Congo, they lead with *Who is your family?* In my case, they asked: Was I married? Did I have children?

Francisca answered on my behalf: "Someone just wrote about Lisa in a big newspaper in the US," she said, referring to an article that Nicholas Kristof had written in the *New York Times* about my complete life makeover and sudden foray into activism for the Congo. "She was engaged, but she had to choose between her fiancé and Congo. She chose Congo."

The family was quiet for a moment, processing this oddity. Then her cousin declared, "So it is like *that* you are a Congolese woman!"

Everyone laughed, except Papa Alexander. He hung back through the welcome. He was thin and upright, with tired but watching eyes, hidden behind the shadows of his well-worn baseball cap and faded, stained blue outfit. He was unassuming and reserved, second in command only to Mama Koko. Alexander had reached the end of his patience with the chirpy talk. He'd waited more than a year to tell his story to someone from outside, someone who could share the family's catastrophic shock. As though impatient with the pretense that anything else at all—anything other than massacres and exile from their land—might be on people's minds, Alexander steered the conversation toward the incident the year prior, when he was beaten by the LRA. It prompted his move into town from the family coffee plantation. He started to tell the story.

My video camera and notepad were tucked away in my bag at my feet. I thought it rude to whip it out too soon, and Francisca didn't prompt me with translation. I didn't want to lose any details. "We'd love to talk with you about it. Can we do it later?"

He agreed, and didn't say much more that day.

But we couldn't stop the current. Everyone else—the extended family packed into the family *yapu*—jumped in to share bits about the in-town attack down the road just days before.

The day of the attack, a few children were collecting water after school, at the community faucet in plastic jugs. They spotted men in long coats with guns. *LRA*. The children ran. The gunmen followed and started shooting. A bullet hit a father carrying his three-year-old. It flew through his arm and pierced his daughter's stomach, blowing her intestines out the other side.

They shot a young woman running with her one-year-old baby boy, ripping apart her genitalia. She collapsed. Grasping the baby, she dragged herself on her back into the bushes to hide.

The United Nations didn't send scouts that night to look for survivors, even though they were only a few miles up the road and it wasn't even dark yet when the attack happened. No Congolese army patrols, either.

In the morning, a neighbor followed the bloody trail to the bushes, where they found her dead body. She had bled out during the night.

Her baby was cradled in her lifeless arms, still nursing.

Francisca's mind was racing—*I don't want to know this*—as brothers and cousins jumped in, talking over each other in a chorus of details.

I asked the family if they knew the mother and baby.

Yes. Francisca's eyes widened when she heard the name.

It was Antoinette, Francisca's cousin.

The Procure

• • • •

The first night of our arrival in Dungu, rusty metal gates pulled away to reveal the courtyard of our new home. After we had heard about the Bamokandi attack, Francisca arranged for us to stay at the Procure de Mission. Just the name of this guesthouse, run by the Catholic Diocese on the more peaceful side of town, conjured images of a charming place, a sanctuary, something a guide book might describe as "spotless" or "nestled" somewhere lovely with "friendly hosts."

It wasn't.

The Procure was a basic brick compound facing inward, wrapped around a dusty clay parking lot. The odd fruit tree stretched up from the ground. The lot was littered with industrial trucks, car parts, and piles of gravel and sand. A lone cement room stood in the middle of the courtyard, a kind of snack bar. Men seemed to lounge and drift in and out all day and night, sipping beer, sitting in stackable plastic deck chairs scattered about in collections of ones or twos or threes. They might chat with Clementine, the hostess who served drinks, when she hadn't disappeared into her staging room for afternoon naps.

I was assigned a dark room, in an annex, next door to Francisca and Mama Koko. When I closed the door, daylight was blocked out almost entirely, leaving a small florescent LED lantern to augment the dreary light bleeding through a cinderblock window slit, set eight feet high on the wall. Dark blue, ruffled gingham curtains with bright embroidery, try as they might, couldn't lift the spirits of the place, with its ubiquitous dust and cement. The generator roared. Francisca asked about a room change for me. With the departure of Procure guests, I was shifted to a neighboring room, brighter with picture-frame windows. It reeked of piss. Not like any urine-soaked bathroom a few weeks behind in the cleaning, but that long-neglected urinal smell, the ferment of piss stacked on top of piss.

The stench couldn't outdo the glory of our welcome-basket treats: an oil drum filled with murky whitish water, like watered-down milk, with floating dead flies and miscellaneous organic matter. Mama Koko, who would be staying at the Procure with us, sat out front sipping a beer while Francisca and I stood in the hallway, contemplating the situation. Francisca broke our silence.

"The water is a little bit . . . not clear. And cold," she said. "Maybe I'll bathe at home."

I was not above bucket baths, even cold ones. I'd taken them many times in India, even in icy Himalayan water. Still, I weighed out going the following weeks without bathing. But the dust and sweat had already done their mating dance, forming a gritty film covering my body.

I set up my toiletries and dashed back to the room. I found Francisca stalled in her doorway, wrapped up in her African cloth, bath supplies in hand. "Decided to go for it?" she asked.

We did a few rounds of "You go." "No, you go." "No please, you first."

I caved and went in, dousing away the grime in a murky-water bucket bath, my mouth firmly closed.

A half hour later, as Francisca emerged, we gave each other thumbs-up and high fives. It felt good to be clean . . . ish.

It was only when Francisca woke up on our second day with Mama Koko sleeping on the floor beside her that the surreal cast of the visit retreated and she felt she was home. As we gathered our things to leave the Procure and head over to Mama Koko's, I noticed the Runner from our first day on the far side of the mission compound. It was perched on a dirt mound, chug-chug-chugging as a group of guys pushed it off. I leaned into Francisca, "That's not the car we rented, is it?"

"That's the one," she said.

We both looked back over at it. The guys were pushing it across the courtyard, trying to give it a running start. It kicked to life.

A quick-starting getaway car was a prerequisite for our trip, even if it meant I needed to spend $50 per day for five weeks. Although the Procure generously offered the push-start guys as part of the deal, I told Francisca flat out: I'm not renting a car that won't start.

Runner

• • • •

So, we rented the car that wouldn't start. It was the only rental car in town.

Mayano, our driver from the first day, a distant cousin of Francisca, picked us up in the Procure parking lot. He pulled Francisca aside: "I didn't look my best our first day. I didn't know we would have a white person with us. That's not the real me." He stood back, arms wide, displaying his new outfit as though revealing a prize: baggy dark wash jeans with lots of extra '80s-style zippers, and men's fashion dress shoes, extra long and pointy. "I like to look a little bit different."

In town, Francisca dashed into a government office to take care of a film permit—a requirement if I wanted to video and shoot photos around town—while I waited in the car with Mama Koko. Mayano sauntered and roamed the yard. His floppy wide-brimmed hat gave the impression he was imitating the strut of some lone hero in an old Western, always with a hand on his belt or pager, ready to quick-draw. He finally wandered back from a food stall and slid back into the Runner, reeking of booze.

I rolled down my windows to breathe.

"I'm not renting a car with a drunk driver," I said as Francisca got back in the car, as though I still had discretion.

"I smell it, too," she said.

I pictured our worst-case scenario: an attack. Our getaway plan a complete fail, with Mayano slurring and stumbling around, grasping his pager, while Francisca and I push the chug-chug-chug Runner, a raging drunk driver hopping in and seizing the wheel.

Francisca didn't have any luck securing the film permit, so we pulled up to The Bureau, as locals called it, the only freshly painted and renovated building in town, fixed up with a trickle of aid dollars. It was the mayor's office and a city hall of sorts, a two-story building with a wide wraparound porch and a flagpole out front. We sat outside, waiting for a meet-and-greet with the mayor.

Francisca had fragmented memories of The Bureau. She and Kevin were married there. It was decorated with impatiens that day. But sitting out front, she pondered the flagpole. When Francisca thought of childhood—the family "castle" in Duru, the corn-husk dolls, the monkeys dangling around the edges of the peanut fields—her memories were tinged with magic. That flagpole, though, was a relic from days she would rather have forgotten—memories that were now her only reference point for what was happening with the gunmen now, and for what a family, what a town, does when it is washed out in bloodshed.

"When I was little, they killed people there," she said. "I saw it once."

The Bureau

• • • •

Young Cisca didn't understand the forces swarming around Congo after independence. She was eight years old when, in 1964, she first heard talk about Simba rebels. Cisca was with her mama Dette visiting relatives out of town when André called them home.

The United States had recently aided the murder of the first democratically elected head of state in Congo, Patrice Lumumba. In a backlash, the anti-Western, Marxist-affiliated Simba militia took control of much of Congo, with the aim of taking over the country. The militia quickly turned on the people, who mostly wanted no part of its rebellion. It aimed not only to kill all white people in the country but also to wipe out anyone who appeared elite or affiliated with whites.

Cisca and her brother rode on other people's bikes along the road to Dungu, passing mango trees and cemeteries, watching the road's packed gravel, so smooth back then that it created a mirage reflecting the sky. Dette peddled at their side with one baby strapped to her back and her bike piled with Cisca's toddler brother along with all their things stuffed into an oversized duffle bag.

A pickup truck and a Land Rover pulled up behind them. Rebels hung off the sides and top of the pickup. Guns pointed out of every window of the Land Rover. The rebels had crowned themselves with palm leaves and wore matching palm-leaf skirts over their trousers, a cheap embellishment for self-appointed kings.

Dette pulled over to the side of the road to let the vehicles pass, pushing Cisca behind her. The truck slowed; one of the rebels spoke to Dette. "Trying to run away from us?"

Cisca hid from his red eyes and hair gone wild.

Dette said, "We hear you are good guys. We were just visiting family."

"Looks like a heavy load on the bike. Why don't you let us take the kids in the car?"

It was not Dette's place to refuse a favor from heavily armed gunmen. Still, she tried. "No thanks. We're fine."

"Give us the address. We'll drop them at your place."

Cisca and her brother climbed in the back of the Land Rover, between big men with big guns, commander in the front seat. The rebels shouted and drummed songs the whole way. Cisca tried to not move. Down the road, a man flagged down the car. It was Kumbawandu, the chief of that area; tall and fat and dressed sharp, he carried himself like royalty. He told the gunmen he was tired of hiding and demanded to talk directly to the Simba leadership.

He squeezed in next to Cisca. She tried not to look at anyone, as the commander hammered him with questions—mostly about his association with white people—while the rebels screamed their songs all the way back to Dungu.

Dette had never peddled so fast, trying to balance babies and bags, saying Hail Marys the whole ride. When she finally reached their shop at the junction, she found Cisca and her brother with André; they'd been dropped off at home without incident.

In the morning, Cisca heard gunshots from the center of town. It was already a routine: Every morning, before the shops and market opened, the Simba started their day by raising the flag in front of The Bureau. Then they executed one, maybe two or three enemies of the rebellion, mostly the educated or moneyed. It usually took only one or two shots.

Not that morning.

Papapapapapa. Papapapapapa. Papapapapapa. Papapapapapa. Pow.

As townspeople filtered back through the neighborhood crying, Cisca overheard them tell André: "The big chief is dead."

Kumbawandu had been taken out to the flagpole, with onlookers gathered around to watch. They told him to lie down, but he wouldn't do it. "I'm not going to let you tie me like a goat in front of my people!" He lunged for their gun, and shot several of the rebels dead before they killed him.

They rolled his body in a barrel to the one-lane Kibali Bridge, next to the manor house, where they dumped him in the river. The current would eventually wash away his body, like all the bodies they dumped over that frilly Belgian archway.

The next day, Dette tried to get the family back to the normal routine. She got up early and had coffee while heating the leftovers for breakfast. She warmed water to bathe the kids before they came to eat. As they did every morning, together, they said one Hail Mary, one Our Father, one Glory Be to God.

Cisca dressed in her blue and white school uniform and met her friends in front of her house for their walk across town. Dette stood at the front of the house, flagging down stall-keepers from

Bamokandi on their way to the market, asking them, "What are you selling today?"

Cisca and her friends passed through the town center, past The Bureau, and onward across the Kibali Bridge. She noticed blood caked over the spot where the bodies of the chiefs had been dumped. It was greasy, too. She wondered if Kumbawandu's body was the one that left the grease stains. He was so big.

The Simba soldiers interrupted class that morning, and hauled the children back across town to The Bureau, with their teachers at their side. The children lined up around the flagpole. Cisca was one row back, but she was tall enough to see, even if she didn't want to. Simba marched their enemy-of-the-day out for execution, already beaten and bandaged. Cisca recognized him: the principal of a neighboring school and a good friend of her dad's. They tied him to the flagpole, as the Simba sang and danced. They asked the audience of captive school kids, "Do you want him to be killed?"

"No," some mumbled.

Cisca's teacher told the girls to pray. Some girls covered their eyes; some put their thumbs in their ears to block out what was to come. Cisca bent her head and stared at the dirt, as she and the other girls began: *Hail Mary, full of grace. The Lord is with Thee. Blessed. . . .*

Gunshots pierced the air before they could finish even one Hail Mary. Girls cried, pee trickled between their legs onto their uniforms and pooled on the ground. Cisca wouldn't look up. Instead, she buried her face in her hands, while they pulled out the next prisoner. It was her skinny chirpy classmate Biroyo's dad, who worked in the school office. Biroyo passed out on the ground when she saw it was her father, before they pulled the trigger. They severed his hands like the Belgian colonists used to do, mounted them on spears, attached them to the bumper of their car, and drove around mocking the children. "Hey, wave hello!"

Cisca couldn't help but see. She held her hand over her mouth and shook, trying to hold it in, but vomit seeped around her cupped hands, spilling down her uniform and onto the ground.

They shouted at the kids, "Go back to school!"

None of them did.

Cisca walked home with her cousin, silent the whole way. The world was so different. Every day, she walked over the Kibali Bridge on her way to school. Even if the current carried away the bodies, there was always more fresh blood on the spot where they threw the chiefs. No one cleaned it. The blood caked and crusted unless rain washed it away.

The grease stayed a long time, long after the blood.

The Simba were out of control, they were killing everything: people, dogs, anything that moved. Everyone in town knew that André, with his scooter, boutique, and history with the Greeks, was a prime candidate for The Bureau. A friend warned them his time at the flagpole was coming. Soon after Chief Kumbawandu's execution, Dette set out with the kids, while André stayed behind just long enough that they wouldn't notice the family sneaking out of town. He left every door and window of the house open, to look like someone was still home, and then slipped out of town unnoticed.

The Mango Grove

• • • •

On the road outside of town later that day, André caught up with
Dette and the children, and they continued until they were about
thirty miles from Dungu. In Kiliwa, they gathered with extended
family before setting off again. Of those who wanted to flee from
the spreading Simba violence, few wanted children with them.
Too risky. Children made too much noise and slowed the group
down. Those who had children stuck with André and Dette.

The family left the road behind them, past the farmers' fields
that clung to the road, out into Congo's bush. André swung his
machete, slicing his way through vast fields of elephant grass
taller than even he was, as Cisca followed close behind. They
passed through fields of grass and scrubby trees, stretches of jungle
teeming with snakes and monkeys, and more fields of elephant
grass. The walk seemed to go on forever.

Then, as if by magic or blessing or both, the dense forest un-
dergrowth opened into a flat, bare patch of ground, without underbrush, covered only with leaves, perfect for a campground. Ancient
mango trees surrounded the campground, their thick trunks and
tops so dense Cisca couldn't see the sky. They were planted in a
perfect circle. The family surmised that someone must have lived
there years before, since mangoes don't plant themselves in circles
in the forest. Nearby, baby cassava tendrils peaked out, fresh, soft
and new, the kind that grows after fires burn off the old bushes.

While the grown-ups built shelters of leaves and twigs to
keep them dry in the torrential rains soon to arrive, Cisca and her

brother found sticks and poked around a nearby stream covered with dry leaves. Cisca's stick wriggled. She lifted the leaves. Catfish! Pools formed under the leaves, and the fish were in water so shallow the kids could reach in and grab as many as they wanted. Dette heard them squealing with delight and brought a basket. The grown-ups joined the children in collecting bunches of fish, which Dette smoked and saved for the long campout to come.

The family fell into a routine. Every morning, they went to the creek to pray to the ancestors and forest spirits, with only special leaves they gathered around camp as an offering. The family gave thanks: *We have nothing to offer. No eggs. But thank you, spirits, for the day, another new day. Guide us. Protect us. If we did something wrong, forgive us.* They sipped stream water and sprayed its droplets through the forest, hoping their prayers would land like the droplets on the leaves, and touch the spirits.

During the daytime, Cisca and the other kids played silently. They were not allowed to roam. The men set traps for antelope. André planted peanuts. They harvested oil from the palm trees. André even made soap. But mostly, the whole family spent all day, every day together with little to do but tell each other stories.

At night, the men took turns with the watch, sitting up with homemade spears should Simba rebels on the run stumble into this place—and of course they also listened closely for the lions that sometimes stalked the camp. Most nights, Cisca chose to sleep outside under the trees, next to the papas on night watch. She wasn't scared, even when she heard the heavy lion breath and low growling just on the other side of the bushes. Ancestor spirits were supposed to be out in the middle of the night, so if she did get scared, she prayed for intercession and drifted back to sleep.

Months passed as the family cocooned in the forest. Cisca forgot they were on the run. She let thoughts of the Simba go. She loved the birds' songs, the crickets chirping, and the antelope that sometimes wandered into camp. Cisca believed that the ancestor-spirits of the creek chose her family. She thought for sure the spirits led them to this sacred grove, and surrounded the family with its force-field of good to protect them. The spirits brought the fish, cassava, palm oil, as if to make it possible for Cisca and her family to retreat to a time when things were pure, untainted by the forces consuming their country—forces that seemed to be squeezing Dungu, squeezing Congo, like dried termites crushed in a sieve for their oil.

Francisca never knew how they heard the news, but they eventually learned that the Simba were ousted and life could go back to normal. After harvesting the peanuts they'd planted upon their arrival in the grove, the family returned to Dungu.

Everything André had built was stolen, broken down, gone. He held off buying replacement household goods such as the nice mattresses they used to have. The family slept on stacks of palm leaves so that André could invest, instead, in restocking the boutique and getting the plantation back to full capacity.

It was a dry year. The citizens of Dungu were hungry for the Simba violence to be washed away with the rains that seemed like they would never come. The town buzzed with plans for a collective early-morning offering to the spirits. Tita Vica was among the elders in Dungu who knew the rituals best. Cisca asked to go with her, and Tita Vica agreed, though she had no plans to wake Cisca. It was a school night.

Cisca slept lightly that night on her stack of palm leaves. She woke to the sound of the white chicken clucking as her grandma Tita Vica packed it into a basket. It was still dark. Cisca slipped out of bed and put on her little sweater to keep warm in the middle-of-the-night chill. It was well before 3 A.M.

"I'm ready," Cisca said.

"I didn't think you were serious," Tita Vica said.

"I'm serious."

"You still have to go to school."

"I will."

Tita Vica wrapped her shawl around her neck, and they left the rest of the sleeping family. Hundreds of people from the Bamokandi neighborhood had gathered at the crossroads in front of their parcel, with chickens, eggs, rice, and other food, to begin the procession.

The crowd began swaying toward the town center. Tita Vica held Cisca's hand as the singing began. A woman's voice rose above the crowd with the twists and lifts of a bird in flight, singing one word: *Baati*. The procession began, with the crowd calling back: *Baati. Baati. Baati*. Cisca didn't know the word, but she figured it was an old Azande call: *Rain come down*.

With palm leaves waving above the crowd, women beating on old plastic oil containers, the procession moved through town toward that spot where all their chiefs had been dumped into the Kibali River. Processions from every neighborhood in Dungu converged on the Belgians' one-lane bridge. To Cisca, it looked like the whole town was there on those banks, in the early-morning shadows, hovering around the abandoned manor house and under the bridge's decorative cement railings. As the dark silhouettes of palm leaves waved above, ladies bundled like Tita Vica lined up and down the banks of the Kibali.

They called to all the good spirits, chanting the litany of names of the ancestors, the chiefs who were killed and thrown in the river, to the spirits of old chiefs, the spirits of the Christian saints, the spirit of Abraham, praying to them all to bring the rain:

> *Here we are. We have nothing. Children to feed. Send us rain. We need to grow. We are looking to you. Don't turn your back on us. This is what we used to do for you. This is what we still do for you. We keep on doing it. We don't forget you. Don't forget us.*

Tita Vica was among the first to step up to the edge of the bridge, where grease that Cisca still imagined was Kumbawandu's remained. Tita Vica made her offerings to the river, tossing the white chicken, bound, into the rushing water below.

Cisca made it home before the sun came up and was off to school on time as promised.

In the late afternoon, she was playing in the yard with her brother when the sky went dark. Cisca listened as wind rushed through the mango trees and bent the palm leaves, like the trees were talking. Like the wind was saying something. Thunder rolled like the harvest drums. Then lightning flashed from one end of the sky to the other, to the limit of their eyes.

Cisca scrambled inside with her brother. The rain came like heaven had opened. Everything dry became wet. The termites came out the next day. From that day, for years on, the rainy season had rain, and the family had food.

Shortcut

• • • •

We wanted to see the site of Antoinette's attack, where they found her body. The fringe of Bamokandi was still a no-go area, at least to most locals. Residents had abandoned the neighborhood and crammed into the homes of friends or family on the other side of town. The few who stayed on lived with sporadic LRA sightings, enough to lead to the popular assumption that the LRA must have set up camp not too far from town.

Our driver Mayano was the one and only way out there, and he seemed to have sobered up since the verbal lashing he got from Francisca over his drunk driving. We had to pay extra-close attention to tell the difference, though. Sober or drunk, his loose saunter and puffery made it hard to tell.

We piled into the Runner at Mama Koko's. After several failed running starts, it puttered to life. We drove a few houses up. Francisca rolled down her window and called to a young man, perhaps in his late teens, with the muscular build of someone who had eaten well most of his life. It was Antoinette's brother. He reluctantly slid into the backseat, agreeing to show us the attack site.

Mango trees sheltered the dusty road out to the UN airbase, where we decided to stop first, hoping to retrace the LRA's tracks into town and perhaps discern how the UN could have missed a massacre in an area it had supposedly secured.

The scent of burning brush grew as we cruised farther out toward the attack site. Parcels gave way to dense, jumbled meshes of vegetation, smoldering as men tried to burn back the grasses and palm leaves and climbers, refusing to give a spare inch of potential cover to lurking LRA.

Farther on still, the compounds thinned.

We looped around the UN airbase like it was a race track. It wasn't hard to understand how the LRA gunmen managed to sneak past the UN fortress and its lookout, surrounded by fields and bush. Not because the forest was so dense, which it was, but because of the UN compound's insular nature. Like an air-tight submarine or a pressurized aircraft cabin, the UN maintained a Congo-tight presence, sealed off from the elements, whatever or whoever those elements might be. How on earth would the UN have known an attack was under way?

As for the Congolese army, a few soldiers hung out on the side of the road, but they didn't patrol off the main roads. The expanse of land surrounding Dungu was open for gunmen of any stripe to mark their new territory as they saw fit, in this case with the bodies of locals.

We cruised back up the road toward town.

Suddenly, Mayano took a hard right, into dense roadside bushes.

Palms and vines and blind corners swallowed us faster than I could grasp what was happening. It must have been an old road, now overgrown and corroded into a single footpath, with just enough grassy shoulder to fit the Runner. Branches enclosed us in a narrowing tunnel, pawing at the windows.

Call it a vibe, call it primal fear. Francisca's skin puckered into goose bumps. We were heading straight into the gunmen's new hub. Their presence permeated the air.

She knew this road; it used to be a wide avenue. An old cemetery sat just on the other side of the bushes, its cement headstones abandoned decades ago. She imagined the LRA choosing that old cemetery as their campground, trying to draw on the power of the dead. She pictured gunmen blocking our way out.

We've got to turn around.

We've got to get out of here.

We're giving ourselves to them.

Still, we lurched forward, revving the Runner engine through crevasses deeper with every few feet forward. *We're swinging at a beehive,* I thought. And if the Runner died? There was no way to push-start even a lawnmower on this rutted-out, overgrown road.

"Let's stop," I said to Mayano, as though he spoke English. Mayano giggled as though we were thumb-wrestling or playing footsie. He thrust the car out of a crevasse and kept plowing forward. I turned to Francisca: "Can you ask him to stop, please?"

She asked. He giggled again.

I looked him in the eye: "Stop the car."

He laughed, as though to say "Have no fear, little ladies—leave it to me!"

The wheel slipped down another foot-deep crevasse, but it didn't break Mayano's seeming delight in riling us up.

Trusting that my tone would say it all, I slammed my hands together in an abrupt line, signaling a wall, and yelled "Stop!"

That, he got.

He thrust the Runner into reverse and backed us out to the main road.

"I was scared back there," Francisca said.

"You felt it too, huh?"

"Bad vibe."

Antoinette's brother had been quiet, but as we drove back toward town, he said, "LRA were spotted around there Tuesday morning." That was just a few hours before we had flown in. "They came down that road and hid in the cemetery watching," he continued. "There were five of them."

"Which road?" I asked.

"The road we were just on."

Impression in the Grass

• • • •

We took the long way around, through a disorienting maze of adobe huts, roads like a rubbed-out sketch of city plans drawn in a more prosperous time, now all but erased. "They used to have street signs," Francisca said, pointing to back lanes turned into narrow trails. The deeper we crept into the neighborhood, the sparer each yard became. Then sparer still. The Bamokandi primary school's brick classrooms were abandoned, classes discontinued. The LRA had marked their territory, as if to intentionally leave a repellant aura and render the landscape empty.

The path rutted out, and the Runner slammed to a halt.

We climbed out of the car tentatively, gingerly, as though softer steps and quieter voices would matter. The area was dusty and open. No smoke, no ash, no people.

We followed Antoinette's brother, weaving through parcels, and up to a tall wall of sticker-bushes. He pointed over it. "She was over there."

"Can we see the actual spot?" I asked.

He motioned us onward. We paused at a crossing, as he pointed to Antoinette's old place up the path.

I pictured her running.

"She was shot there, and came this way." We followed him away from her home and traced her course to a spot a few feet off the path, splayed in the grass, where she had dragged herself to hide, grasping her baby, waiting for the sun to set.

The grass feathered out in the shape of her body, her impression clear with the imprint of her head and outstretched arms and legs. Like mini-graves, two small piles of sand marked the spot where she bled to death from her wounds.

"They put the piles of sand to cover the blood," her brother said.

Francisca stood back, too sad to stare, or to stand too close. *What have I gotten myself into*, she thought, looking away. She didn't want to see the face of Antoinette's brother, afraid she would cry. She thought about Antoinette's deflated breast, the oxygen draining from her. She didn't want to be there anymore.

I stood over the spot where she died.

I pictured her hours after she saw the dreadlocked gunmen, in the middle of the night, left behind, clenching her baby. Did she watch the sky, the silhouettes in the grass? Did she know she was dying? No one was coming to help her. She must have known that. She gave her baby the only thing she had to keep him from wriggling and fussing and getting himself killed: her breast.

What was the baby feeling those hours after Antoinette had slipped away? With his mother growing cold, his ploys for comfort unmet, what panic took hold as he was trying to move her stiffening arms, or squeezing her limp breasts? What was it like for him with the morning light coming, neighbors hovering above him, scared to pick him up?

Bystanders left him on her body until the family came, as though his little soul might be haunted, like his misfortune might rub off.

I filmed, as if the lens could remove me from this place, make it less real. I turned to Antoinette's brother, who was trying to be elsewhere.

Francisca said, "He never wanted to come here again. He only came because we asked."

Sensing his pain, I asked him: "Is it difficult for you?"

I only heard him say *mercy*, one of the few words shared by French, English, and Lingala. But the remote look in his eyes, his effort to hold it together, was unmistakable.

He said, "Yes, I'd like to go, please."

Gunshots

. . . .

Mama Koko began retiring early most nights during our time at the Procure. Francisca rolled out a mattress and piled thin blankets for Mama Koko on the floor of their dark room. Francisca laid on the metal bed above, and they stayed awake late, talking until they drifted to sleep.

The unspoken question—perhaps the unspoken premise—of our visit hung in the background through our time in Dungu, especially those nights. *Will this be our final time together?* From time to time, Mama Koko would say to Francisca, "I'm happy you're here. But I'll be happier the day you leave. At least I'll know you're safe."

One night, gunshots woke Francisca. It was at a distance, from Bamokandi maybe? Mama Koko's parcel? She lay silent, listening. Her thoughts raced. *What happens if we have to run? Lisa can't go to Bamokandi. The UN, we'll go there. . . .*

"Cisca, are you sleeping?" Mama Koko whispered.

"Did you hear that, too?"

Mama Koko had. Another gunshot cracked in the distance.

A priest passed through the Procure, calling out "Alert! Alert! Be prepared!"

Francisca tensed. *How long do you wait? When do you run? Where do you go?* It occurred to her that Mama Koko and the family had lived with this question nearly every night for the last year and a half. Francisca said, "We need to get Lisa."

"Don't. Her spirit is at rest," Mama Koko said. "You can't

wake her with bad news. It harms her spirit. The priest will knock
on everyone's doors if we need to leave."

"When this happens, what are we supposed to do? Are we
going to run?"

"Jesus is bigger than these people. Your dad, your brothers
and sisters, the ancestors will intercede for us," Mama Koko said.
"Nothing will happen."

Through the small cinder-block slit eight feet up the wall,
they heard footsteps and men's voices from the street, just outside
the mission.

Mama Koko said, "God is big. Keep praying."

"What about the family?" Francisca asked, thinking of her
brothers, her baby nieces and nephews.

"Give it to God."

They prayed the rest of the night.

Francisca's brother Gamé came at first light. Several versions
of the story had already circulated around town by breakfast, all
involving drunk Congolese soldiers. One had a bad dream or shot
off his gun while sleepwalking or fighting over a girlfriend.

At breakfast, Francisca decided to ask me, "Did you hear it
last night?"

"Hear what?"

Hospital

• • • •

Francisca asked an old physician friend to take us on a tour of
the Dungu hospital, only a few blocks from the Procure. Under

yellow-washed cement chambers with high ceilings, filled with rusty beds and plastic mattresses, we met LRA victims. Most had been there only a week.

Many of the patients were from the town of Bangadi, part of the Red Triangle, as the UN called it, the epicenter of LRA activity to the north. Many men wore thick bandages covering machete wounds on their skulls and backs, a twelve-year-old girl had been rescued by the Ugandan army just before being made a "forest wife," and another young woman, who held a baby on her hip, took a bullet through her ankle and had dead eyes that said it all.

We didn't ask.

Francisca seemed anxious and disturbed by the time we got back to the Procure for our 4 P.M. curfew. As I sipped Coca-Cola and Mama Koko had her beer, Francisca didn't want to talk. We hadn't asked, but still, her doctor friend came by to show us photos documenting the LRA victims' injuries. He squeezed himself in tightly between Francisca and me while scrolling through the photos.

A man's back, with five bullet holes doused in iodine. A three-year-old girl shot through her stomach. Some of the images were so close up and gory that they seemed like abstract paintings of fleshy holes, shattered bone exploding like fireworks through a bloom of flesh.

With each new photo, Francisca gasped.

Mother with child, covering her mouth with a cloth. Then the cloth dropped, revealing a fleshy hole around her gums and teeth patched up with crude stitching. The LRA had sawed off her lips.

"Oh! How could they do that?" Francisca blurted out.

The doctor continued through his slideshow, photo after photo of faces with ragged holes where mouths used to be, but Francisca was done. While she cried, I asked for copies of the photos on a thumb drive.

I had only ever known a Congo where limbs were hacked off and fed to children, where women had the "look of utter death" in their eyes after being raped. That was the noticeable difference between Dungu and South Kivu. In the Kivus, the war had raged for more than a decade; some kids in their teens remembered nothing else. Shock there had gone numb. In an emergency, the life-and-death stakes can only go on so long before they seep deep into the psyche and become their own kind of normal. You can only scream for so many hours, so many days, until the vocal cords fry. People in the Kivus grew to expect the brutality, and I did too.

But no one in Dungu was acclimated to the violence. No one there knew of the world that watches lion-breathed militia snag Africa's young with the same curiosity and detached pity that one watches antelope devoured in nature specials.

And if the locals weren't acclimated, then Francisca was a year and a half behind even that curve. The fresh wounds on a child felt as if they'd been inflicted on her own daughter. To her, Congo was home; these people were her neighbors. Violence was not inherent to the landscape of her Congo—mango trees were, and the fragrant air after a rain.

We'd only started on our project, just days into what was to be five weeks of a packed interview schedule, and already Francisca was hungry to retreat, to cocoon with her family, to be absorbed with crazy aunties and familiar fingers braiding her hair, as though she could find her old home still there, if only I would stop asking so many questions.

Perhaps I had a leathered heart, toughened from so many war stories, but with only five weeks in Congo, I didn't have the luxury of slowing down. On a normal day in South Kivu, I was on the road interviewing people eight to ten hours a day. My focus was on leveraged impact. We had to do Francisca's family justice.

The next morning, as we ate in the dimly lit Procure breakfast room, Francisca asked, "So when are we going to be done with these visits and interviews?"

Mama Koko's War Tribunal

••••

Word got out around greater Dungu that we were talking gunmen at Mama Koko's. The should-be dead—the ones who saw the LRA and lived—showed up, one or two at a time, lingering in the *yapu,* hoping for an introduction and an invitation to offer testimony. We coined them "Mama Koko's War Tribunal." With each new guest, each new story, each set of shell-shocked eyes, another little chunk of home as Francisca knew it crumbled away.

We tucked ourselves into Mama Koko's dim, bare-cement living room. A faint smell of must mixed with aromas of Congolese food lingered from lunch or drifted in from the kitchen out back. Delicate baby-blue flowered curtains were drawn tight over wooden picture-frame windows. A coffee table with a lime-colored tablecloth separated the two wooden armchairs from the three-seater wooden couch, each pillow with a different cotton cover in mini-florals or purple paisley. It was already late January, but a shiny accordion-style Christmas banner still hung beside a window, below a bees' nest that had survived the Congolese army takeover of the house. An any-minute evacuation was always possible, so the family stopped fixing the place up each time they moved back in. This time they left the leviathan-bees almost the size of my thumb to haunt the corners, swoop across the room, and dive at our heads as we stitched together the story of the family's encounters with Kony's gunmen.

I figured we'd start with the most recent attacks and work our way back, and since Antoinette had died just a few weeks before we arrived, we'd start with Modeste, Antoinette's dad and grandfather to the still-nursing baby. He was the first to sit with us privately.

Papa Alexander followed us into Mama Koko's living room and sat on the opposite end of the sofa, seemingly put off that we hadn't yet gotten to the story of his LRA beating. I didn't know yet that half of Alexander's family had been murdered and abducted.

Modeste spoke with barely audible tones and restrained hands, as though paralyzed with shock. He had been at home at the time, just a few houses up the road, taking care of some of the grandchildren while his daughters worked. He heard gunshots, then screaming. He grabbed the two little boys. Along with everyone else in Bamokandi—thousands of neighbors—he ran toward the Dungu Bridge, toward town center, hoping to reach the UN for protection. By the time he reached the narrow bridge over the Dungu River, Congolese soldiers had blocked it. It was the only escape route.

Blocked? I paused to clarify.

Papa Alexander shook his leg, anxious, poised to jump into the conversation.

Modeste explained: The army lined up across the bridge with guns pointed at the thousands of people trying to escape. They were told they couldn't cross. But if the attack was in progress less than a mile away, I asked, why didn't the people cross the river elsewhere or just wade across? He said, "The water's deep. We can't swim."

Alexander couldn't hold back anymore: "If we tried, the Congolese soldiers would shoot us like we were the rebels."

Modeste and other folks from Bamokandi slept that night around the warrior statue and roundabout, corralled as though in a holding pen.

"It's not right," Modeste said, shaking his head. "The soldiers should be in the front, with the people in the back, so *they* can protect *us*. But the soldiers were in the back and we were up front with the LRA coming."

At daylight, a boy found Modeste among the crowd and gave him the news: Neighbors had found Antoinette's body, and left her baby in his dead mother's arms until the family arrived and her sister pried the little boy away.

Modeste boiled. "I can't even talk to my own government. Because they don't care about the way people are dying from the LRA. They don't do anything about it."

A few days before, Modeste had marched with his fellow citizens through the center of Dungu to protest the Congolese government's failure to protect. "I would ask [our president] Kabila: Why did I vote for you? Everything that is happening to us, you don't do anything. We don't even hear your voice. You say nothing. You don't care."

I asked, "It sounds like you blame the Congolese government and the Congolese army for what happened. Is that right?"

The question was directed at Modeste, but Papa Alexander couldn't contain himself. He said, "Yeah, it's like that."

"Yeah, it's like that," Modeste echoed.

Papa Alexander said it again: *Yeah. It's like that.*

Superman Paul

. . . .

Like Modeste, Paul was a survivor. Despite his missing four front teeth and his bald head, he looked eighteen. It turned out he was thirty-three. His innocent eyes made him look much younger.

The day he came by, Francisca and I didn't notice him sitting to the side, unassuming, lost in the steady flow of Francisca's relatives who floated in and out of the *yapu.* Hours passed as Francisca visited with family at Mama Koko's, and finally, someone introduced him. He wasn't another cousin, not related at all. He knew Francisca's cousin Bernard and was there when Bernard died on October 31, 2009, just a few months before our arrival. After our belated introduction, we slipped inside the living room and Paul began to tell his story.

Food was the problem. It had been more than a year since the attacks began. Paul's parents had already been killed by the

LRA, so he was taking care of his twelve orphaned brothers and sisters. The whole village was hungry, but people were too scared to go to their fields, abandoned in the LRA's wake.

Francisca's cousin Bernard helped organize forty-five farmers to make one last trip to collect their crops. The willing ones among them broke into groups of ten.

Paul was in Bernard's group. They had known each other for years, swapping farm labor the way good neighbors do. Bernard was like that: a stand-up-and-take-charge sort of man.

The group split into pairs, headed out to the fields, and collected crops without incident. The problem came on their way back. Their neighbor Patrick saw a boot track in the mud. It wasn't a familiar boot track. *No regular Congolese person wears shoes like that,* they decided. Patrick knew what it meant.

He ran back to the place where Bernard's group had agreed to meet, hoping to warn the others. But once everyone was gathered and began sorting out their getaway plan, Patrick insisted on going back. The thing about Patrick, Paul explained, was that the LRA had *already* burned his house and stolen everything. All he had left in the world was a piece of plastic given to him by an aid organization that he used for a tent. But as soon as he saw the boot track that day, he ran, leaving behind all his crops—and his makeshift tent.

He wanted that plastic tarp.

He went back out to the fields, this time on his own. The tent was gone. That was the moment he knew they were all dead.

This time Patrick came back slowly, quietly, feeling the weight of LRA eyes on him. By the time he got back, it was dusk.

There was no time to escape. Paul and Bernard knew the LRA were somewhere, right there, watching. The ten from their group crowded under the open straw hut and lay down for a long night. They tried to sleep, as best one can when you know you are being watched, when you know you'll be killed at first light, when you know it is your last night on earth. The men were silent, except when someone asked for a cigarette. Paul noted to Francisca, "We were human, after all."

In the very early morning, a hard, driving thunderstorm came down. When the first light peaked into the hut, they gathered their things and set out.

They walked in the open, along the road. Paul walked in front. He smelled cigarette smoke. He wasn't smoking. He turned and looked at his neighbors behind him. They weren't smoking. Paul stood still. So did his friends. He scanned the bushes. Nothing.

The tip of a gun stuck out from the grass.

Then he saw a boot.

And a cigarette.

The LRA didn't move. Paul pointed and the farmers all ran, scattered, without knowing if the LRA was chasing them.

Paul ran back to the meeting spot.

Why didn't he just keep running? Why not save himself? They were his neighbors. They were his family. *You don't just leave people*.

Paul met up with the other nine members of the group. Each had fled back to the meeting spot at the hut, including Bernard and Patrick, the one who had gone back for his plastic tent. They walked together, the ten of them. In the fields, the ten farmers saw ten men in Congolese army uniforms. The gunmen called out, pretending to be Congolese army. Some of the farmers ran away, and didn't look back. But not Bernard, not Patrick. Not Paul.

The gunmen approached them, speaking strange Swahili, broken and odd. They weren't from around there. One of them said, "Sit. Sit."

Bernard and Patrick knelt down in the road. Paul did not.

The gunmen tried to soothe them, blessing them with the weird Swahili, as they cocked their guns. "Sleep. Sleep. Don't be afraid of death."

They shot Patrick in the head.

Bernard's hands were on the back of his head. They shot him through the chest. His arms flew in the air. Paul could still see it, the way Bernard fell backward, arms flying.

They hadn't noticed that Paul didn't kneel. He stayed back, still. But now it was his turn. One of them barked, "Who do you think you are? Superman? Get over here."

Paul ran. Bullets flying, the gunmen stayed on him as he ran through the forest and fields, fast. He ran past huts, screaming warnings to people so they could run, but without breaking his pace. He kept running and running and running until he was on a road. He lost the gunmen. He must have gone in circles, because he saw his own bike. He jumped on and rode and rode and rode. He doesn't remember much about that ride.

In town, they wanted Paul to go back to show them where to find the bodies, but they all saw his shock. *He can't talk*, they said. *Give him some time.*

Villagers found Bernard's body. His chest was split open, cracked wide, empty.

"Stop! Oh, stop!" Francisca cried in English. This was her cousin Bernard. She didn't want those images in her head. She had heard about LRA rituals, the ones where they ate people's flesh. In a flash, she imagined Bernard's empty chest. She thought someone must have eaten her dear Bernard, the strong man who used to ask her dad about Francisca: *How's your "boy"?* Boys were supposed to be preferred, of course; girls were thought to be a waste of time. André always praised Francisca for being faster than any of the boys, though, and Bernard would echo André: "Your dad is right about you. He loves you very much, and we love you, too. You can do anything."

Francisca said, "It's too much."

Over the weeks, other survivors came often: former teenage "forest wives," elderly men, ten-year-old child soldiers. They each had a story worthy of volumes. As we listened, my friend's warning rang in my head: "If you see the LRA, *you're dead.*" Looking into the eyes of each survivor felt like witnessing a walking miracle.

Sometimes, when the survivors told their stories, Francisca thought she would throw up. But she had to be there. She was among the only English speakers in town, and the survivors were willing to talk to me mostly because they knew her as a local. She stopped looking them in the eyes. If she looked, she cried. Better not. She stopped looking at their faces, trying to avoid the pangs of empathy. Instead, she tried to shut it off by thinking about the calls Joseph Kony was making to his commanders on his satellite phone. *Can't they trace those calls? How hard is that? How many satellite calls are trekking to space and back from the middle of the Garamba National Park? Where is the world?*

Papa Alexander still sat close by and jumped in now and then, offering impatient commentary on other people's stories. He asked, "When do you want to hear about what happened to me?"

A Knock on the Door

• • • •

As *the days went on*, Francisca dutifully translated, absorbing the stories, but she was saturated. She got tired of explaining to her friends and family members: "If Americans know what Kony is doing, they will care. They will want to do something." Did she still believe it? She didn't know—it all felt too vague. She explained to me that she wanted something more concrete, more tangible to do—a real-world project—that would help the people of Dungu.

So, in between interviews, we scouted out potential projects. First we stopped by a women's sewing cooperative, then a local health clinic, hoping we might be able to arrange medical supplies. On the way out, we paused by an elementary school.

"I helped start this school," Francisca said in passing. For a moment, she lost herself in the memory, back in the days when she was a single mother of three young children, in the early 1980s.

Everyone who knew the town gossips—and that was everyone in Dungu—knew things hadn't worked out between Francisca and her kids' dad. Late-night callers often circled; for months, their uninvited knocks on her door kept her awake almost every night. From the time the knocks started, she told the men through the closed door to go away. Instead, they hung on for hours, begging in hushed tones.

She retreated into silence, not a word, not a crack in that door. Most often it was the henchmen of the chief, who already had five wives. He sent police to try to collect her for his night-time pleasure.

Francisca did not find a trace of flattery in the endless late-night knocking. She knew where they were coming from. *They think I'm a thing.* So the men circled, sometimes until 2 A.M., when she was trying to rest up for her job across town teaching at the new pre-school she was helping to found. On the school's first official day of classes, it was just Francisca teaching two of her children and two children of the couple who asked her to establish the school. Within a week, they had so many students that they moved into a classroom at the Canadian Brotherhood's monastery.

One day on the four-mile trek home from her new job, police arrested her, claiming "justice must be done." Justice, they insisted, had to be negotiated at the chief's private residence. Francisca declined to take the police up on their offer to negotiate her release. Instead, she opted to wait them out in jail. For hours, she ignored their endless nasty jokes and offensive questions. When she was released at the end of the day, she asked the Diocese if she might barter extra work around the mission in exchange for living on the school grounds, to escape the harassment, and the late-night knocks.

Francisca took on sorting piles of "lift and throws" or "rotten person's clothes"—used clothing from America—alongside her friends. One day, Francisca's friend pulled out a massive pair of men's underwear, teasing Francisca: "These belong to your future husband!" They knew an American Peace Corps volunteer was supposed to arrive soon, and her friend was trying to buoy Francisca by convincing her she was going to marry him.

Pure silly, Francisca thought, because, as everyone knows, no normal man would want a woman who already has three children.

The night the American was due to arrive, his host—a neighbor who lived across the street from Francisca—was out of town picking up fruit for the cooperative. Francisca and her friend volunteered to stay up to greet the new resident.

By the time the SUV pulled in, it was far after dark. Francisca strained in the harsh headlights to see the emerging lanky, baby-faced American with long blonde hair. She blurted out, "Bonjour, mademoiselle!"

"Hey, I'm a *man!*" Kevin was barely twenty-two years old and not exactly straight-laced. More of a wannabe hippie, he was hungry for any alternative to becoming a company man.

The night they met, he was fresh off a four-day ride by truck from Kisangani to Isiro, followed by an all-day truck ride from Isiro to Dungu. They showed him to his room. Eager to get acquainted, he stashed his stuff and came back out to talk. Kevin and Francisca stayed up for hours visiting in that brick house with its corrugated tin roof.

Over the following months, during shared dinners and group conversation, Francisca tried to ignore Kevin's gaze lingering on her. He found Francisca beautiful and, most of all, confident. Negotiating at the market, hanging out with friends, in front of her class, she carried herself like a leader, a big sister, like a woman in charge. It took several weeks for him to figure out that the three children she lived with were in fact hers, and that she was four years older than he was. By then, he didn't care.

Sometimes Francisca spotted Kevin working on his first project, a retaining wall by the river. He was always dressed in grubbies and working alongside his guys. One day, she asked, "You coming for lunch?"

"Why would I take lunch? They don't go for lunch," he said, pointing to his impoverished crew. Francisca hadn't seen that before. She mostly saw white bosses who wore nice shirts to work, sat in their office, and told people what to do. She was especially surprised when she passed by the worksite later and saw him divvying up roasted peanuts and doughnut holes between himself and the crew for lunch.

Kevin fell in love with Africa, his home next to the river, the giant acacia tree next to the house, the pride in filling buckets of water from a well he had dug himself. He biked out to remote villages to work, on back trails, through deep mud puddles, sometimes twenty-eight miles out of town.

On one of those early evenings, he asked Francisca to go for a walk. Francisca didn't trust men. And she didn't find white men all that attractive—the ones she'd met were all goofy show-off types. But Kevin was handsome, no question. She liked his tone of voice, steady and direct. She agreed to the stroll.

On the walk, he asked, "Are you seeing anyone?"

"I have three children!"

"My father married a woman who already had children."

Kevin was different. He proved honest and offered an unheard-of level of respect. No public displays of affection? No problem. She had to go to church, or didn't want meet up some days? Then that's how it was. No drama.

In an era when Belgian ex-pats sent their wives back to Europe so they could freely pluck through Dungu's slender young girls as though they were toothpicks, this sandy blonde man patiently, diligently courted Francisca. He visited her every day at her school, during her break, when he brought her snacks of fried bananas and peanut butter.

Francisca confided in Mama Koko and asked her to size him up. So Mama Koko showed up at snack time at the school to assess this American. As she left, she gave Francisca her unambiguous verdict. "He's not a hypocrite. He looked me in the eye."

Francisca's dad, André, was another story. He didn't believe Kevin would stay for the long haul. It was bad for his daughter, and bad for his family. Francisca was embarrassed. She avoided introducing the two for years.

After three years, and two extensions of his Peace Corps service, Kevin wanted to stay on. He wanted something serious, and asked Francisca to move in with him. Instead, citing the children, she moved back to Mama Koko's compound, which a constant rotation of thirty-plus relatives called home.

Kevin returned to America for a six-week vacation, promising to come back. Every week, a friend from the Procure delivered postcards for Francisca from America, with pictures of things like whales and bridges, and always the line *I think about you every day.* Every week, she heard the motorcycle coming, and knew more postcards were being delivered, along with her friend's taunts: *Does this guy ever sleep? He writes you all the time!* She kept them on a stack by her bedside, reading and rereading secretly in her spare time.

One day, Francisca was working over the open charcoal stove at Mama Koko's when her sister Justine whispered, "You have a visitor."

Francisca looked up. Kevin stood in Mama Koko's yard, strapped down with an oversized, frameless backpack stuffed with hefty reads like *The Seven Mysteries of Life*, *Monopoly Capital*, and *The Development of Economies*. His arms were overloaded with bags, his red work boots dangling by a string.

Francisca just stared at him.

He finally prompted her. "This stuff is kinda heavy."

Francisca pointed to her mud hut, with a dirt floor. "That one is mine."

Home

• • • •

Most of Dungu accepted me as quasi-family, by virtue of Kevin's reputation, which had hung on for twenty years after he and Francisca left. Francisca introduced me around town as his sister. From time to time, before she could divulge the official story, a long-lost acquaintance or "other cousin" approached us on the street: "This is your daughter, all grown up?! How good of you to bring her!"

It was the first and only time I was mistaken for Congolese.

Francisca sometimes heard people talk about us nearby, loud enough for her to hear. "If that's Kevin's sister, then things might really change around here. He's the kind of white person who gets things done."

Francisca was nervous that any mention of activist, author, or media would lead people to believe that money was flowing to her family when it wasn't. But the charade grew more awkward one night when I went to check my e-mail at the Canadian Brotherhood's Internet café. An older Canadian monk approached me, asking, "You are Kevin's sister?" Before I could answer, he said, "I have something to show you."

He pulled out his laptop, which stored old films of Kevin building houses in Dungu in the early 1980s. He was so young then—only twenty-three or so—and looked like a member of the brat pack gone lost in Africa. His name inspired respect, perhaps because he'd stayed so many years, and not in the Belgian part of town. They all said so. *He wasn't like other white people. He stayed on everybody's level.*

The day Kevin showed up with all of his earthly possessions in his overstuffed backpack, boots dangling by a string, he moved into Francisca's hut and started eyeing an abandoned adobe house on the property. It had four bedrooms, but the roof had been eaten away by termites. When it rained, water ran down the walls. Kevin replaced the roof, patched the walls, and repainted.

Soon they had a lovely four-bedroom place with a sitting room and a dining room and an open floor plan appropriate for young children.

Chatter around town swelled, even among close friends. The standard refrain became *What are you doing with a white guy, he'll leave you*. Francisca knew how these things could go: Her best friend was living with a Belgian who had shipped his wife and kids back to Europe to make space for his young Congolese plaything.

Kevin and Francisca spent time around other American and Belgian-Congolese couples hoping to avoid gossip. They went to parties in Little Belgium often. One week, when Francisca stayed in because she wasn't feeling well, her friend told everyone Francisca was pregnant. *And you know Kevin's not happy about it. That's what Kevin told me. He didn't come to Congo to have some baby. He's pretty sure it's not even his.*

Francisca was pregnant, and kids weren't their plan. By then, she was throwing up at random times nearly every day and had missed a couple of periods.

Francisca confided in Mama Koko, who already knew what everyone was saying. Kevin-doesn't-want-it-even-if-it's-his rumors had spread through town overnight and arrived at Mama Koko's along with the town gossips for morning coffee. Mama Koko shut them down. "If the child is black, it's my grandchild. If the baby is mixed, it's my grandchild."

Mama Koko counseled Francisca. "I know you. You know yourself. Don't worry about it." As for Kevin, "You live with him. You need to talk to him and trust what he says."

Francisca told Kevin that night.

Kevin was normally a quiet guy. But when Francisca told him about the baby, he couldn't hide it—he was thrilled. He asked: If the baby is a girl, could we name her Natalie?

Kevin spent his free time working fine wood into a crib, and every day when he came home, he asked, "How is Natalie today?"

Who's Natalie? the family wondered. They didn't name unborn babies. Nor did they prepare with baby goods, for fear of a stillbirth. But when Francisca was six months pregnant, Kevin came back from Kinshasa with two suitcases full of baby *everything:* extra mosquito netting, baby powder, lotion, clothes, diapers, soap, and a beautiful fabric for Francisca to make herself a dress to wear home from the hospital, with a set of elegant gold earrings to match.

A few months later, Francisca went into labor when Kevin was out. Mama Koko walked her across town to the hospital. When Kevin got home and heard, he ran straight into the maternity section. It was time. Kevin scooped Francisca up from her bed and carried her into the delivery room, fussing and making sure everything was in place: Was Francisca comfortable? Did Mama Koko have a nice chair? How about a massage for Francisca's feet? *Breathe, Francisca, breathe.*

A woman in labor a few beds down had been watching them. She screamed at her husband. "You see that! What the hell is wrong with you! I should have married a white man! That is love!"

They had a boy, Isaac.

When Francisca came home, Mama Koko and her aunties took care of everything, as was the custom. New mothers were expected only to breast-feed, snuggle the baby, and rest. Kevin rallied the guys in the family to take over cooking and cleaning on the weekends to give the women a break. Everyone was in. The guys took pride in their hearty meals and dish-scrubbing skills, until male neighbors started to show up, complaining that this type of behavior would do nothing good for their own domestic situation. Their wives were already talking about it, so please knock it off.

Kevin brought home more beautiful fabric from Bunia for Francisca a year later, when she was pregnant with their second child, though he asked her not to wear it yet. When Solomon was born, the congratulations went on for weeks. It confused Francisca enough to ask: "Why do you keep congratulating me? You already saw the baby."

"Your upcoming marriage!" her friends said, which was weird, since as far as Francisca knew, there were no wedding plans. News was all over town, on account of the government-issued notices posted on the mango trees throughout the town center announcing their marriage: *If anyone objects to their upcoming marriage March 30, 1989, speak now or forever hold your peace.* But Francisca had been hunkered down at home with Isaac and baby Solomon hadn't seen the announcements.

That night, Francisca asked Kevin, "What's all this talk? Are we getting married?"

"Yes!" he said, with a huge smile. He was planning it as a surprise, making all the wedding arrangements. The fabric he had brought from Bunia for a dress was meant to be her wedding dress, a wax-block print pattern with oversized blue and gold lotuses.

He could see Francisca's reservations, so he held her. "We've already been married all these years. It's just legal. Just making it official. Did I need to ask you again?"

"Let's do it!" she said. "But no P.A." Public affection, that is. She still had a rule about it.

Kevin had already written Francisca's dad about the traditional arrangements. When André arrived from the coffee plantation, Kevin showed proper respect by asking two of his Congolese friends to stand up and make his case. In matters of marriage, men didn't speak on their own behalf.

Normally a big dowry was expected for a first daughter's marriage, but the family already loved Kevin. They didn't need lots of livestock or money, so Kevin made a small donation for the sake of tradition. They formed a small procession consisting of all the kids, André and Mama Koko, brothers, sisters, and onlookers from town, Francisca in her beautiful wax-block print wrap, and gold earrings to match, as they made their way to The Bureau, decorated with impatiens for the special occasion.

All the aunties ogled, since men don't usually plan weddings in Congo. Kevin had arranged everything, including palm leaves interwoven with bougainvillea strung around the yard. He served chicken, fish, goat in sauce, roasted peanuts, and fried plantain. They borrowed a car battery to plug in the cassette player, and danced to Congolese music, mixed with the occasional tune by Earth, Wind & Fire.

In the distance, rain clouds gathered and threatened a downpour over their outdoor reception, so a group of Francisca's aunties slipped away to the back of the house. They tied potato leaves on their heads and around their waists, chucked an axe at the ground so it stuck upright, poured ash in a circle, and danced, invoking the ancestors. *Our first daughter is married today! Don't dishonor us to let the rain fall and disrupt our celebration!* Then one of the aunties pulled up her skirt and shook her bare buns at the east, as aunties were wont to do on big celebration days, or really any occasion their spirit-summoning skills were needed.

They came back around the house and assured Francisca: *Carry on. It won't rain.*

And it didn't.

America

• • • •

America. They never meant to stay. They had planned a life in Africa.

With two new babies and the three kids Francisca brought to their union, Kevin decided it was time to graduate from the Peace Corps' volunteer wages. He decided a degree in engineering would be their ticket: With a master's degree, he could comfortably support a family, do meaningful work, and they could live in any corner of Africa. All they needed was a couple of years in America for graduate school.

During their final evening walks in Dungu, Kevin coached Francisca on what to expect, from the street sweepers scrubbing the roads with water to the bright city lights.

Francisca knew to expect huge buildings. She didn't expect that America would make her feel so small.

They arrived in Seattle in the winter. Kevin's parents greeted them, taken aback by Francisca's flimsy cotton outfit. It was far too thin for blustery Pacific Northwest weather. "How could you let her come here in something so light!"

"It's what she wears," Kevin said. He loved Francisca in a bright wrap, just like the day they met.

"She's cold!" his dad said, bundling her in his puffy coat.

Kevin's step-mom took her shopping the next day. Francisca wore bright colors that made her stand out, not darks. She didn't want to blend into her clothes and disappear. No one would notice her. Francisca scanned the boutiques for patterns, colors, flowers, anything with hints of home.

No such luck. In a dressing room, Francisca found herself draped in a muted dark-purple woolen plaid jacket, with a matching skirt that hit below the knee.

"You look so good!" her mother-in-law said, trying to buoy her.

I look so stupid in this thing. How on earth am I going to dress like this?

"It will keep you warm," her mother-in-law said. Francisca hated it, but she had only just met her new in-laws. "Yeah, it's good."

When they moved to Kevin's hometown of Portland, Oregon, Kevin worked all day and studied his engineering texts late into the night. Francisca hated being dependent, but she couldn't even figure out how to grocery-shop on her own.

Francisca knew only a few words of formal British English she'd learned in school, like *Good morning, sir. Good afternoon. How do you do?* She was lost with this American English: *Hi. How you doing?* Or *What's up?* (She wasn't sure what that meant, but she was sure it was very aggressive.)

She was too shy to speak more than a little here and there. Some people were patient. Others peppered her with questions, choosing to not hear the words through the French accent. *Excuse me? What was that you said? What's that accent? Where are you from? Excuse me. What's that? What's that? What's that? I can't follow.* She would repeat and repeat and repeat herself to selectively deaf ears. Sometimes she would escape to the bathroom to cry.

Francisca's hair was growing into an Afro that she could no longer get a comb through. She attended a neighborhood church on Sundays, and noticed the minister's wife had lovely, comb-able hair.

Francisca abhorred makeup, or anything fake, really. The thought of chemicals on her hair was a radical move, but she wanted to fit in, and she had noticed that ladies didn't wear Afros in America. The minister's gracious wife connected Francisca with another parishioner who specialized in black hair and agreed to do Francisca's for free.

On the way into Kevin and Francisca's modest rental home, the hairdresser made sideways comments that landed funny: *Nice place. . . . What are you doing living here?* By morning, clumps of hair stuck to Francisca's comb. Her hair was falling out. Humiliated, Francisca wrapped her clumpy, balding head in a scarf and went to church anyway. Francisca showed the minister's wife the box she'd fished out of her bathroom garbage. "But this is for white people's hair! She knows better," the minister's wife said.

Francisca skipped church on Sundays from then on.

Francisca felt like she was shrinking. Kevin could see it. Francisca the leader, the one who owned the classroom, who haggled at the market, was slipping away. They made plans to get back to Africa.

In 1994, after finishing graduate school, Kevin was offered what appeared to be the perfect job in Rwanda, stationed in the resort town of Gisenyi, a lush hill town overlooking Lake Kivu, right on the border with Congo. Their new life was a dream combination of both of their worlds, one that left Francisca and Kevin scratching their heads, wondering *What the hell did we do right?*

Kevin's job came with a freshly renovated lake-view house on a hill. To Francisca, it was paradise: whitewashed cement and brick, huge glass windows, lavish flower gardens, room for a vegetable garden in the back. The house came with a staff of five—a cook, cleaning lady, gardener, security man, and a driver—all of whom made Francisca uneasy. The cook stayed out of the kitchen because Francisca handled all the family meals.

There was just one problem. Along the ninety-some-mile drive to Gisenyi from Rwanda's capital of Kigali, they had to pass through thirteen military checkpoints, and even in the resort town of Gisenyi, people on the street seemed closed off and tense.

The day after their cargo container arrived with all their things from America, the phone rang at five in the morning. It was Kevin's colleague: "You guys are going on vacation right now. Pack the car."

The Rwandan president's plane had been shot down, igniting long smoldering ethnic tensions between Hutus and Tutsis.

Francisca peeled back the beige curtains in the living room and saw that the road out front was covered with Hutu militia who would come to be known as *Interahamwe,* "those who kill together." Kevin and Francisca woke the kids, quietly slipped them into their car, and drove to the border of Congo. The soldier at the checkpoint stopped them. "Where are you going?"

Kevin played it cool. "We're just going to see her family."

"Do you have a letter of permission?"

"No."

"Then you're not going. Nobody's leaving."

They went back home and pulled the blinds tight, staying inside, listening to gunshots coming from the nearby hills, trying to calm themselves down. Was it really so radically different from where they had lived in northeast Portland? In their neighborhood back in Oregon, three kids within a two-block radius had died from stray bullet wounds.

But as the morning went on, the gunshots grew more frequent, and closer.

Bombs exploded nearby, shaking their glass windows.

Then came the bloody screams from the university just behind their house.

Kevin and Francisca pulled mattresses onto the floor, up against a wall, as far away from the windows as possible, to avoid shattered glass. They lay there, trying to reassure the children, trying to tune out the gunshots next door that killed their Tutsi neighbor.

Their cargo container in Kigali was left behind, including all of Francisca's family photos, along with everything in their home. Francisca bundled up a few changes of clothes for the kids, and they left. Their car crawled through the deserted streets, passing men with machetes. When they finally arrived at a UN office, other foreigners had gathered. Kevin insisted they stay in their car, away from the crowd, in the event of a bomb.

Armed men showed up. One with red eyes knocked on Francisca's door and motioned for her to roll down the window. As she lowered the glass between them, the *Interahamwe* hovered a few inches from her, dousing her with his putrid breath. He spoke Kinyarwanda, presumably to discern if she was Tutsi. Francisca understood none of it. Kevin interjected, "Can you speak to her in French? She's from Congo."

The guy moved on.

Finally, word came that Congo would accept the foreigners.

Decades later, Francisca's memories of Rwanda have a break here, a break there. She doesn't want to remember. This was the site of the most concentrated period of ethnic cleansing in human history, a 100-day genocide during which between 500,000 and 1,000,000 Tutsis and moderate Hutus were slaughtered by the Hutu majority.

Francisca and Kevin tried to move back to Kigali after things calmed down, but rumors circulated that Kevin had visited the wrong friends in Kenya. The new Tutsi government that had ousted the *genocidaires* decided Kevin had been a collaborator with the *Interahamwe*.

After months of passport struggles, they finally made it to America with all of the kids, except for Francisca's oldest son

Jean, then a teenager, whose father wouldn't allow him to leave Congo. She had to leave him behind.

In Portland, Kevin was offered a permanent position at an engineering firm. At their antique dining room table, it was decision time: Go back to Africa, or build a life in Portland. Francisca pulled each of the kids aside and asked, "You remember, don't you? Do you really want to go back *there?*" *Not me*, the kids agreed. Kevin called for a family vote: Get a career-track job in Portland, or go back to Africa!

Kevin's was the lone vote in favor of returning to Africa.

Their dream retreated into the corners of their craftsman bungalow, into the carefully framed African prints and cloth work, into the figurine reminders of the life and the family they had left behind. Francisca was left with the daily pangs of missing Jean and Mama Koko and the rest of the family. Kevin never returned to Africa.

Mama Koko's Retreat

• • • •

Mama Koko waited until her private time at night, long after everyone at the Procure had gone to bed and Dungu had gone quiet, to tell Francisca about the day in September 2008 when the LRA attacks started. The day that Francisca set up the cheese bar while her family buried Roger's body. The day before the phone calls started.

Uneasy murmurs had been circling in Dungu about the LRA gunmen. They'd killed a couple of people in the market. People began to pass through, fleeing into town, saying it was getting bad up north, that the gunmen were coming.

The family decided that Francisca's brothers Antoine and Gamé would make an emergency trip to the fields along with their wives, to harvest what food they could ahead of the oncoming panic. They set out on their motorbikes, leaving Mama Koko at home to look after the children.

That day, the trickle of villagers from north and west of Dungu swelled, flooding the area near Mama Koko's, warning the bewildered townspeople that they were out of time. The reports picked up as the day went on. Attacks occurred closer and closer to Dungu. Too close. Everyone from Bamokandi grabbed their bundles of food and cooking pots and crossed the Dungu River, then the Kibali River, in a mass exodus to the south.

Mama Koko weighed the situation as the children played around the dusty *yapu*. She was responsible for all the family babies, five of whom were under five years old, with only a couple of pre-teen nieces to help. They had only so many hands and backs on which to strap the babies. But the neighborhood was sweltering with panic.

Mama Koko didn't pause to load up supplies for an evacuation. She gathered the children and ushered them across town to a friend's house. They spent the night. In the morning, she hoped to slip back home to get some supplies—sheets and a pot for cooking. But the road into town was blocked. Then she heard gunshots.

She had to get out of town. She had to find Antoine and Gamé. She grabbed her grandbabies and joined a caravan of villagers walking south, heading to her family fields, hoping to find her sons and make a plan from there. She walked a long time, coaxing and lugging the little ones, coaching the teens, trying to listen in on updates from neighbors in exodus.

Mama Koko and the children finally arrived at the family fields. Her sons weren't there.

People passing by the fields paused long enough to tell her it wasn't safe for them to stay. She, too, knew that they had no choice, that they had to keep going. To where, she had no idea.

It was such a long walk, so hot, and dragging the children was so wearying. They didn't have a cooking pot, or even water. They were all so thirsty. They walked straight into the middle of nowhere. Twilight set in.

Mama Koko scouted a spot in the bush off the road and rallied the children to pile leaves into a bed, where they huddled together, and slept.

In the early morning, Mama Koko stood and felt the weight of it all on her sixty-nine-year-old bones. There was no choice; they had to continue to flee. They set out for another day. But she was dizzy. The world swayed and Mama Koko collapsed. The girls couldn't rouse her. She lay on the ground, unconscious, surrounded by panicked, weepy teens and screaming grandbabies.

Water splashed on her face. Strangers hovered over her. She was still on the road, children's cries around her. Passersby had doused her with what little water they had. She pulled herself up, and they kept going.

A small church parish gave them food that night, and let them sleep inside. The next day they set out again.

Antoine and Gamé frantically combed the refugee-filled roads on motorbikes, trying to guess what route Mama Koko might have taken with the children. Finally, they spotted her. The shattered brood piled on the motorbikes and made their way to another family plot farther out.

On the edge of a rice field, the family collected palm leaves and wove them into walls for a hut, with a plastic tarp for a roof. It wasn't at all like when Francisca was a girl, when they were hiding from the Simba in the mango grove. Back then, André came back from the bush with bags of peanuts. *The bush was our bank,* they would say. But in 2008, the LRA owned the bush—no more bank. This time everyone was in hiding, every family with their own secret spot. People missed the harvest.

The family stayed for months. Mama Koko spent most days sitting at the corner of the hut, fighting off pneumonia, looking at the rice field, watching the sky.

One day, she heard a loud noise, like thunder. She looked up and saw fighter jets shoot through the sky. Then the boom of the bombs. *Good. Kony must be dead,* she thought.

Families inched out of their hiding spots, speculating that this must be the end of the LRA and it was time to go home.

When they finally made it back to Mama Koko's parcel in Bamokandi, everything was gone: no shoes, no cooking pans, no sheets. They surveyed the damage, as the parade of shocked neighbors, friends, and cousins began, everyone swapping updates—who lived, who died, who hadn't been seen in a long while.

It was only a few weeks before they had to flee, again.

Papa Alexander:
The First Sitting

••••

We'd been in Dungu a couple of weeks before we sat down with Papa Alexander. In Mama Koko's dim living room, Papa Alexander settled himself on the far end of the couch and removed his worn baseball cap so we could see his eyes.

Even though Papa Alexander's wife Mama Cecelia was the one who washed Roger's wounds that ill-fated September day in 2008, Roger was not Cecelia's son. He was not even the child of one of Papa Alexander's many other wives but, rather, his firstborn son, from way back in the 1960s, when Alexander was known around town as André's handsome younger brother.

As a young man, Alexander bypassed the local farmer's daughters and family friends. He fixated on Neseti, whom he had found in his beer-hazed evenings among the young and restless of Duru. She was the kind of girl all the guys wanted to get alone, and Alexander did.

Francisca was a pre-teen when Neseti started coming around. She stood out, and not in a good way. She was pretty, but *Lord, was she loud*. Talk, talk, talking all the time. And she smelled. She was a smoker, not of cigarettes but of stinky water-vapor pipes made of bamboo.

Neseti's charm thinned, even for Alexander, after baby Roger's birth. She slipped out during evenings, late, then later still, leaving Alexander to watch sleeping baby Roger and to soothe his cries while listening for Neseti's drink-heavy footsteps. One night the blue light of morning made it into the hut without Neseti making it back.

A day passed.

Another day passed.

And another day went by with the baby crying long and hard in Alexander's arms, as his new single-dad reality dawned.

Neseti eventually reappeared a few days later. It was no surprise when she announced she'd met another man and would not be back. Fine, but Alexander was not prepared for her to leave town with baby Roger, not to be heard from again. Yet, that's exactly what she did.

Alexander had no more luck with Sako, who moved on shortly after the birth of their baby girl.

From then on, when it came to women, Alexander decided to keep it simple. Simpler than love. Simpler than lust, even. He liked to entertain. He needed help around the house. And he had money. With the cold eye of a project manager, Alexander collected wives.

Ngalagba was a great cook.

Monokoko kept a tidy house.

Toni made good coffee.

Cecelia was an afterthought, a refugee from South Sudan whom he had spotted around town. He had the dowry on hand, so he made an offer. She rounded out the team with her needle-craft and crochet.

Between the early mamas and the four wives, Papa Alexander's brood swelled to twenty-six children. The decades passed, marked by harvest feasts with André and Dette and long evening talks with the children around the fire. Aside from the sporadic grief of losing infant children, life was good.

Francisca had watched Alexander's wives as she moved through her young adulthood. Toni was tall and beautiful; she laughed plenty, but she never harvested much. As all the other women went to work in the field in the morning, she would wake up and sit a while.

One morning, Francisca saw her bring water to Papa Alexander to wash his face, without the usual kit. He tried to prompt her. "Where's the soap and towel?"

"Why don't you ask your other women to get you soap?" She marched back into her hut, emerged with the bar of soap, and threw it at him. "Or get it yourself!"

As he got up to leave, he said, "I don't know what your problem is, Toni." She followed him with her fist.

Monokoko was quiet. She kept a perfect house, pressed Alexander's shirts, and watched most of her children die in infancy from weak-blood diseases.

Ngalagba, for the most part, stayed drunk. She didn't care about much of anything, but hid away, drinking. She stumbled around the courtyard, slurring, as if no one knew what was wrong with her. They knew. They all knew.

Cecelia was beautiful, and clean like Monokoko. Young Francisca always liked her the best. She'd had an education and often asked Francisca how her schoolwork was coming along.

Alexander never forgot about Roger. He talked about him all the time, looked for him for years, asking around about Neseti. No one knew where they went.

Francisca entered a teachers training program, and by the age of eighteen she was ready for her first job, working for a school. Little did she know it would lead the family to rediscover Roger.

Francisca was a single mom, of baby Jean, when they transferred her to Gilima, a town about thirty miles from Dungu. She moved into a simple mud-and-grass hut on a compound for teachers. It had two bedrooms and a little patch of land out back, perfect for a garden. She added pineapple bushes, onions, potatoes, and cassava.

At school, for their annual botany lesson, Francisca's class joined another one in the courtyard, huddling around a tree to learn about root systems and photosynthesis. A stir rose up in the back of the class and one of the students piped up, pointing at Francisca: "Désiré says that teacher is his sister!"

"Liar," someone said.

Francisca's fellow teacher laughed, opening the door to rounds of taunts, booing, and shouts of *Liar!* More mocking rumbled through the crowd.

Francisca approached the ten-year-old boy. He looked terribly familiar. In fact, he looked exactly like a young Papa Alexander. She asked, "What is your name?"

He was imploding with shame. As he opened his mouth, even in his first syllable, she could hear Papa Alexander's voice.

She cut him off. "Are you *Roger?*"

The boy had been watching Francisca since she arrived as a new teacher a few weeks before, but he was too shy, too scared she would reject him just like his mom always said Alexander had done. Even though his mother had renamed him Désiré, he knew his real name. He nodded.

"Papa has been looking for you!"

"My mom told me he didn't want me."

"Not true," Francisca said, wrapping him in her arms. "We've been looking for you for years."

Right then, in front of the whole class, little Roger's lifetime of imaginary rejection crumbled. He broke down, sobbing in Francisca's arms.

Alexander came to Gilima as soon as he heard. He tried to get Neseti to let Roger go back home with him, but she wouldn't allow it.

A few days after discovering Roger, Francisca spotted him pacing back and forth on the road in front of her yard, trying to look casual.

"What are you doing out there?" she called out. "Come on in!"

As soon as Roger stepped inside, single working-mom Francisca didn't have to ask for his help: He jumped right in, volunteering to draw water from a nearby stream with other boys, recruiting baby Jean to go with him to the back garden to collect cassava for dinner. What with the low-tech cooking equipment, his extra hands were a godsend, whether they were pounding peanuts, grabbing some onions from the backyard, holding the meat while she cut, or carrying baby Jean around on his shoulders. From then on, Roger stopped by often, several times a week sometimes, as much for a good meal as to avoid going home.

Francisca could see that Neseti hadn't taken to motherhood. She drank and still smoked that bamboo pipe. The smell of smoke had settled into her body, her shiny complexion turned to a dull ash. She hit Roger, and her boyfriend was no kinder. Francisca was happy to provide him a refuge. As often as Neseti would allow Roger to escape to Francisca's without a scene, he would.

Roger constantly asked about his long-lost family. *What do you think my dad is doing right now? What's he like?* Always steering the conversation toward the real question on his mind: *When are we going to visit them?*

Just as Dette was surrogate mother to Alexander, Francisca ushered Roger into his young adulthood. After four years, though, when she got a job offer back in Dungu, she scheduled her departure. She wanted to live close to Mama Koko and the family again. On Francisca's moving day, Roger hitched a ride out of town and never looked back. He moved in with Papa Alexander and stuck close for the remainder of his life, rarely farther than a few miles away from his dad.

When Roger was old enough, he sidestepped the party-girl trap and moved in with a regal church-going local, Marie. They remained in Duru, near the coffee plantation, and Roger opened a little shop of his own.

War flared across the border in South Sudan in the 1990s. André, Alexander, and the family had to abandon the coffee plantation to flee the mass of refugees. When they finally emerged from hiding, Alexander surveyed the dried-up trees, the coffee beans stunted and gone to wild, the fields overgrown to bush and brambles. Dette didn't want the coffee plantation. The land was wrecked, raided, broken to fruitless nothing. Alexander decided to reclaim it.

Ngalagba had left Papa Alexander for another man ten years before. Monokoko opted to stay in Dungu to help out with her grandchildren. Toni was not up for the tedium of manual labor. That left Cecelia, who dutifully returned to the coffee plantation and shared the daily sweat with Alexander and the boys, though her hands were now wrinkled and her skin withered.

It took years but the land did come back, yielding a coffee fortune beyond anyone's hopes—especially those of Toni, who then begged to join them. Papa Alexander told her *Don't bother.* Clearing and trimming, fertilizing and constructing, Papa Alexander rebuilt the family coffee empire on André's land with Mama Cecelia—with most of his sons and daughters, their spouses, adopted children, and dozens of grandchildren at his side.

Life was not just good. Life was better than ever.

Until the day they brought Roger's body home.

Who Are You With?

• • • •

There were only about twenty or so white people in Dungu the February of our visit. For the most part, we avoided them. But a few weeks into our trip, a French UN higher-up spotted me on the street, and stopped us. "How long have you been in Dungu? You haven't come by. . . ."

We decided to log a cursory visit to the UN compound at the center of town, a sterile white outfit made up of portable offices in shipping containers, sealed to hold in conditioned air.

Signing in with security at the UN gate, we bumped up against a common problem. Every time we had crossed an international border, checked into a hotel, or signed in with security in a guarded compound, obligatory forms asked: *Who are you with? What is your function?*

It was weird enough in the US, answering endless questions about how I supported myself as a volunteer, the independent nature of my work. But in Congo I was met with blank stares, confusion, and often flat-out dismissal. The strangeness was exacerbated by the fact that I wasn't sure I knew, even secretly, what my "function" was. As we filled out the entry form at the UN, as so often before, Francisca looked at me puzzled. "Who *are* we with? What is my *function?*"

Admittedly, even back in the States, I lingered in unnaturally long pauses on the blank lines next to "Home Address." I started to resent it. As in, *Back off, bucko. Enough with the 'Home Address' bias. Not everyone has one, okay?*

In Congo, the "Marital Status" field also held a mocking tone. I had to check the only box that applied: *Célibataire.*

I'd tried it all, but none of my pat answers worked here.

After a few rounds of this, Francisca and I agreed, between delighted chuckles, on our new answers. Who are you with? *Myself.* What is your function? *No function.*

Eventually we were let into the compound, figuring that our American passports had done the trick.

Inside the air-conditioned offices, we met a mix of foreign and Congolese aid workers from the handful of NGOs in town, all there for a meeting. In pre-meeting chitchat, a scraggly European man described a new project he was developing: only a few million dollars to build a road circling the perimeter of Dungu, so the UN and Congolese army could use it for safety patrols. He drew the road project on scrap paper for us. *That means the LRA would still be here,* Francisca thought. *Roads sound permanent. We don't need to plan for the LRA long term.* (Later that day I showed the sketch to Francisca's brother Antoine, who crumpled the scrap-paper map and handed it back. He said summarily, "Get rid of the LRA.")

Another aid worker told us that the estimated number of remaining LRA soldiers—not including abducted children, but true commanders, leaders, believers—was fewer than a hundred, perhaps as low as sixty. The UN source suggested that official estimates were higher, for fear the international community would de-prioritize a response. My takeaway was the exact opposite, in that eliminating a hundred remaining core LRA fighters seemed like a manageable task.

Francisca and I filed into a small conference room and sat against the wall. The Europeans and Americans took their seats at the conference table, while most of the Congolese crowded in the corners or stood silent against the walls. It seemed to Francisca they'd learned a long time ago that speaking up would get them nowhere.

The discussion was conducted in French, so Francisca periodically whispered a rough translation to me. Even without French, it was easy to track, having narrowed to a debate between the Frenchman apparently in charge and a Congolese man advocating for investing in rebuilding the court system and prosecuting rapists.

The Frenchman spoke the universal language of contempt. He rolled his eyes and exchanged knowing glances with the fellow foreigners, followed by variations on the standard French frowning and a pucker of the lower lip with a breathy sputter: *Ph! It is not poss-ee-ble.*

Francisca watched, noting that he didn't ask questions, especially "What do you think?" *There's another one,* she thought. *What does he base his decisions about aid on, if he doesn't speak with people from here? How can you help me if you don't know me?*

But the Frenchman thought an investment in rebuilding the court system in Dungu was ludicrous. And what he said went.

The Mango Tree Riots

• • • •

"We won't have mangoes this year," Mama Koko mused, as we lounged on our stoop at the Procure—our daily ritual after arriving back from our self-imposed 4 p.m. curfew. "Normally they're already the size of my thumb. But the flowers just bloomed and dried up. No fruit."

She paused, as though reading an oracle. "It's going to be a hard year."

Food was on everyone's mind. It was time to prepare the fields for the year's planting. Following the LRA sightings on the outskirts of Dungu, everyone with land even a mile outside of town, especially to the north, mentally traced their route and calculated their odds. They had all pondered how fast they could run, who and what they would leave behind in that split second, should they see the dreadlocked men. They had all weighed the risk-and-regret equations, chewed the roulette fruits in their sleep. Would you die for a few piles of beans? Bushels of cassava?

No, they would not clear and plant in the coming weeks. The markets were already dusty and bare, mostly with shiny white garlic in mesh packaging imported from China, along with some piles of salt, scattered peanuts, cans of oil marked "USA," or oh-so-sweet pineapple on a good day, if you got there early enough. But little more would be coming. That meant hunger for most of the year.

Earlier that morning, Francisca's brother Antoine picked me up from an Internet session at the Canadian Brotherhood's building with an announcement: *Bad news*. Something about tree cutting. I couldn't quite make it out. When we arrived at the Pro-cure, Francisca was waiting. Odd, as she was supposed to have left for Mama Koko's an hour earlier. She greeted me. "Last night, there was an incident."

At Mama Koko's and throughout the neighborhood, down-time conversation had centered on gunmen, in their varied uni-forms, those UN boots that would not step out of their vehicles onto Bamokandi ground, those lips that would not part to smile at their children. All eyes tracked the Congolese army soldiers from elsewhere in Congo who caressed their teenage daughters with one hand but would not step off the main road to patrol, and would not raise their gun other than in late-night drunken squabbles or, on the odd day, when they herded the locals like cattle for slaughter, blocking their escape from an attack. And everyone eyed the dusty plumes kicked up by the smooth-riding, air-conditioned United Nations SUVs.

Each resident of Bamokandi had been left to stew. Each resident of Dungu had privately asked themselves, *Who is on my side?* Not the ones in the SUVs. Not the ones in Congolese army uniforms. Not one of the gunmen.

A popular rumor wove its way through Bamokandi: *The gunmen are all on the same side. The United Nations secretly sponsors the LRA, giving them food, supplies, uniforms.*

That morning, the neighborhood was abuzz, with a new variation on that theme.

The story had already filtered through layers of Bamokandi residents who saw it with their own eyes, or at least knew someone who knew someone who definitely saw it with their own eyes. The story on the prior day's incident went like this: An off-duty Congolese army officer and his wife noticed a United Nations vehicle carrying six armed civilians. He followed the car and watched as it stopped. Civilians piled out of the back, armed, next to an entrance to the forest, at the same spot where LRA gunmen were sighted over the last few weeks. The Congolese army officer who was watching yelled: *LRA!*

Every nervous Bamokandi ear had stayed trained for that call, poised for the cue of another attack.

According to the witness, the men climbed back into the vehicle and sped off.

It was just the spark needed to concretize the rumors. Locals now had proof: *The UN was sponsoring the LRA.*

Bamokandi dwellers choked with rage.

Men got their machetes. Their spears. Their guns. They took to the streets. As though to spit on thoughts of the future, they chopped down whole mango trees and laid them across the roads for miles, blocking all United Nations access, stoking each other: *If they won't protect us, we'll protect ourselves.*

They covered the entire stretch from the UN airport through the attack area, up the road past Mama Koko's, all the way to the bridge into town. When Francisca heard, she felt sick: *Destroying the mango trees! They are killing the future. Even if one person survived this whole LRA thing, what would they eat?*

Congolese army officers fueled already-wound-up residents with coffee and cigarettes, encouraging them to stay awake all night. In the center of town, crowds gathered in protest and things continued to heat up. Francisca's brother peered out of the front of Mama Koko's house throughout the night, scared that it could get ugly fast.

At some point, the United Nations officers fired shots.

Stoking the standoff, the Congolese army fired back.

Francisca's family insisted that we stay at the mission in lockdown.

I tried to no-big-deal the tension, focusing instead on unbraiding Francisca's hair. But Francisca was shaky. Her mind drifted, mapping out a safety plan. *What will we do if this gets out of control?* Normally, she'd take us both straight to the UN. Today, though, the UN was the enemy of the people. Being seen out and about could trigger attacks against me, if people mistook me for a UN operative.

We'll leave everything and run. What do we really need? Only our cameras and passports.

We'll hide. But what about Lisa's bright white skin? Mine will blend into the shadows. Hers will glow, even far away, in the forest.

I could rub her down with ash, all over her face and arms to make her dark, for camouflage. Then we could slip into the bush behind the Procure, and make our way to the forest next to the airport.

We would hide out until we hear a plane land. Then I'd sneak out and try to convince the pilot to fly her out.

She decided not to tell me about her escape plan until much later. She didn't want me to worry.

By midday, the center of town was flooded with Congolese soldiers, while UN helicopters flew back and forth from the town center to the airbase.

We spent the day hanging around a hot cement hallway in the Procure. I analyzed the rash on my hand. I sipped warm bottled water, trying to avoid the harsh sun and my cave of a room, and texted updates about the riots for my mom to post on Facebook.

Francisca and I kept our eyes on the parking lot, waiting for senior community leaders to pass through and give us periodic updates. Mostly all we heard was, *The situation is tense.*

The mayor told us, "It's big."

By evening, community leaders had passed through the Procure, admitting defeat after a day of negotiations. The UN had dismissed the incident as an invention of the Congolese army. It turned out that the chain of rumors started when a Congolese army officer had simply seen UN soldiers wearing new uniforms and mistook them for LRA. The UN failed to clarify the true story for a couple of days—a clarification that would have tempered the backlash.

"The problem is that the Congolese army is known to make up stories to provoke upset," another community leader added, looking shaken. "They know exactly the right buttons to push."

It seemed to work. For the remainder of our trip, I never heard anyone complain about the Congolese army's failure to protect them. Not one more time.

To make the most of a lost day of interviews, in the late afternoon we slipped over to the hospital nearby. In a dank, urine-stenched children's ward lined with rusty metal beds, we met Francisca's cousin Heritier, the still-nursing baby, Antoinette's boy.

Limp, with grief-stoned eyes, Heritier had been in the hospital for weeks, drained and refusing to rally, despite blood transfusions. It wasn't that he'd been physically injured in the attack. But, the night in his dead mother's arms had *left him cold*, as they all said. *He caught cold.* That cold seemed to have a vice-grip on him.

Heritier's dad dutifully hovered over him, somber and long-faced. I took some photos of Heritier, who struggled to sit up.

"This is my other cousin!" Francisca blurted out. Sure enough, baby Heritier had a neighbor. Half of Dungu seemed to be Francisca's "other cousin," and the children's ward was apparently no different. On a broken vinyl mattress a few beds over, a twenty-something mother cradled her firstborn and only child, also a baby boy. This other boy was fragile, pale with wasting arms, with disproportionately wide eyes as in those sketches of aliens, with the look of one foot out of this world. Francisca visited with the young mother, while I dotted her baby's fragile arms and legs with butterfly stickers. The gifts elicited no more than a glance at the stickers and a stare at me.

I moved back to Heritier, placing a couple of stickers on his hands, too. He looked confused. I could only offer perfunctory condolences. Hoping to help the boy, on our way out I slipped Heritier's dad twenty dollars.

Ash-Like Snow

• • • •

The day after the mango tree riots, the governor of Orientale Province stepped in, declaring that the real problem was the mayor of Dungu. The locals needed a villain and the governor knew that he had to make someone—anyone—responsible for the incident to pacify them. Firing the mayor did the trick.

The riots subsided the next morning, but Bamokandi still smoldered.

Keen to see the remnants of the machete-wielding rioters, we trailed after the air-tight UN SUVs resuming their morning commutes between the air base and town, as locals cleared the downed mango trees from the road.

At the cusp of town, Mayano pointed to a Protestant mission. "They saw the LRA this morning."

We pulled into the brick complex, all but abandoned save a few groundskeepers and a minister. Now, this place was what I had pictured from the sky over Congo, this was what I had imagined of Le Procure de Mission: *spotless* and *nestled* into grassy rolling hills.

As we stepped out of the car, the air crackled and gurgled with fire. I looked up at the hazy sky. Ash and burnt grass drifted in the air like snow. Smoke rose in a ring from the ravines encircling the mission.

Francisca scoped the place out, imagining from behind what tree or road or field the LRA might surprise us. As was becoming a habit, she mentally worked through our getaway: *The river is close by, through the forest. I know the fishermen in the area who keep canoes. We could run through the forest and catch a canoe back into town. Yes, that would work. Most white people—if you say "Run!"—wouldn't just run into the bush. But Lisa, she's a runner. She runs in the forest. If I say "Run!" she'll run through the bush.*

Groundskeepers led us to the far end of the hilltop and pointed into the forested ravine, a jungle dense with ancient trees and climbing vines. The LRA were sighted there the night before in the underbrush, a big flashlight in the trees and darkness.

"How did you know it was them?" I asked.

"We could see their flashlight," the groundskeeper said.

"But how did you *know* it was *them*?"

"It was them."

There wasn't much more to say about it. This Protestant mission was in the inauspicious position of being the last compound before the bush, teetering on the edge of town. If anyone was going to receive LRA visitors, the mission was surely it.

Walking back to the car we saw, from a distance, a group of men emerge from the burning ravines. They had weapons.

I tensed.

"Local defense," Francisca said.

The label wasn't soothing, given the rioting, threats, warnings from leaders to stay away because locals might take out all of those frustrations on a foreigner, even with Francisca at my side. In fact, I'd never run across a militia that didn't consider itself some form of "local defense." Given the explosive riots and the ominous sight of any and every machete I'd seen in Congo, I could only assume "local defense" equaled menacing and bloodthirsty.

They called to us. We stopped. They moved closer. Their bulky male forms seemed to shrivel and their weapons came into focus. They were downright rickety. Closer still, and my tension drained to heartbreak as the four approached. A bean stalk of a boy, no more than thirteen years old, held a home-made mini-spear. A shy-ish, slender man wore a homemade slingshot around his neck, and carried a bow and arrow set made of twigs and twine. The third man held a metal spear almost his height. And then there was the white-bearded, sixty-something school principal, to whom they'd assigned the most deadly of their weapons, a rusty machete, presumably to bulk up the meekness suggested by his utilitarian school administrator uniform. They'd spent the whole morning burning the ravines and fields around the church, to eliminate potential hideouts for LRA gunmen.

Francisca thought: *There's our protection. If the LRA show up, these guys will take care of us.*

What was the master plan of these mad rioters, rushing to the defense of their people, charging the front lines? I struggled to see it. What exactly would they do when an LRA loomed over them or their neighbors with an A-K or axe? Sting him with a hand-chiseled spear? Shoot an arrow from the bow, taut with frayed twine? Slingshot him?

These were Dungu's few good men. Stacked against the UN and Congolese army's meager stores of valor, they were certainly the best and bravest. Based on the desperation in their eyes, I'd guess they would have burned down the whole Congo basin forest if it meant smoking out the LRA.

Burnt grass had sliced streaks on their sweaty arms and pants, and left charcoal crisscross markings on their faces. Ash drifted through the air in swarms, burnt and lost, like prayers caught in some crosswind.

"What do you want?" I asked. "What do you want the world to know?"

"We need peace," one of them said. "Stability."

We walked back to the car, now dusted with ash that had settled on the hood and windshield. One of the men called after us. "We don't want cornmeal! What is that stuff, anyway?"

Reception

· · · ·

A *couple of days after the riots,* we resumed our interviews back at Mama Koko's. Francisca and I held court at the *yapu* as neighbors and family rotated in and out. Whenever we emerged from interviews, Mama Koko pulled Francisca aside and let her know who had stopped by for a visit and how long they'd waited to greet her. She relayed how insulted and angry they were when they left without so much as a hello.

Francisca was torn. She'd already floated the idea of wrapping up the interviews ("enough of this LRA talk") and dedicating the rest of her time to the family. I was annoyed, and tried to remind Francisca of the reason I was spending my scarce funds on the trip, that the interviews and research were essential and meant to be support for her family. Francisca in turn tried to explain to the family that this trip was different, but they didn't get it.

"Can't you just ask your friend for more free time?" Mama Koko asked. "Why don't you just tell her you can't do any more? We'd like to visit more with her, too."

I tried to give them space. Francisca and Mama Koko took alone-time during our evenings and pre-breakfast hours, while I paced the dusty courtyard at the Procure, waving my cell phone at the sky, checking for reception.

Occasionally, maybe once an evening, two or three bars appeared and the phone pinged me with texts and e-mails. The messages were mostly from my mother, fretfully asking if we'd made it home that day.

I slept with my Blackberry, tossing around all night, drenched in sweat. I woke up often, fishing around in my gritty sheets for my phone, hanging over the side of the bed, holding the phone at just the right angle as though it had an antenna, to see if any messages had arrived.

Considering the fervor of my preoccupation, one might think I was anticipating urgent business messages, or notes from loved ones back home: a boyfriend, husband, family. But I wasn't fooling anyone in Dungu. My status as a soon to be thirty-five-year-old *célibataire* was transparent.

I wore African-style dresses almost every day. It was my only option, after tossing to the side my sticky, head-to-toe black cotton, so misguided for these parts. The traditional dress attracted many a suggestion that went along these lines: Kevin took a daughter of Dungu to America, so wasn't it only reasonable that his "sister" should be married to someone in Dungu as the family's gift back to Congo?

When the governor of Orientale Province fired the mayor, he flew in a replacement, a district administrator from another area of the province. He'd landed in Dungu with no more than a wrinkled suit, without knowing why.

Officials dropped him at the Procure with welcome gifts of a toothbrush and a track outfit for his down-time. We felt sorry for him and greeted the new neighbor with idle chatter about politics and the state of education in Congo. By way of introduction, he showed me photos of his wife and kids and admired my traditional African wrap dress.

He was up front. "Marry me."

"You just showed me photos of your wife and kids!"

"You know . . . as second wife."

African polygamists don't usually stir feminist sympathies. Yet, compared to all the American men who cheat, or just want to get some, shall we say, *alone-time* in exchange for as little emotional baggage as possible, I found something refreshing and forthright about the offer. Like, "Yes, I'm married. And I still want in your pants. In exchange, I'll take care of you for a lifetime."

I declined, but thanked him for the generous offer. Of course, should I ever decide a polygamist union in remote central Africa is for me, it's always good to know that a girl has options.

At Mama Koko's, I tried to create space for the family, and filled my time covering the children in stickers and leading them in rounds of camp songs. One of Francisca's cousins, an unmarried teen mother, tried to soothe me. "Don't worry. You'll have your own."

I smiled politely, aware that this was the sort of comment that in the past had set my inner feminist grumbling. *Please. I'm doing meaningful work! Get tied down? No thanks!*

Instead, these days, the comments landed with a disquieting twinge.

I looked away, not with an eye roll but with embarrassment. To be alone, to have no one to lose, was to the Congolese perhaps the worst possible fate. For all the turns of misfortune Mama Koko and her family had suffered, they felt sorry for *me*.

Aunt Harriet

. . . .

At lunch in the family dining room, Mama Koko gathered her skirt and plunked a many-times-reused plastic bottle on the table like a punctuation mark.

Francisca interpreted, "There's been a death in the family."

The bottle was filled with yellowish local liquor, meant to make the pains of death go down easier at the family wake. The baby boy we met the week before at the hospital had died that morning.

"Not Heritier?" I asked, thinking of the boy limp on the hospital bed, gripped by cold from the night in his dying mother's arms.

No, it was his wide-eyed neighbor from the children's ward. The other cousin's little boy. Embarrassed by my inexplicable relief, I asked, "Can we buy flowers for the funeral?"

Francisca laughed, "There are no florists in Dungu!"

But she said cash was always welcome. I trailed behind Mama Koko's procession of family women bearing their local brew, en route to the funeral a few blocks away, deeper into Bamokandi's back alleys.

A few houses down, an elderly woman called to us from under an ancient mango tree. Her arms and feet bare, she was cradled in a traditional woven chair; her hair was in a bundle of short braids pointed at the sky, like a dancer's fingers twisted upward. With a sober expression, she craned toward us to reveal a bandage on her chest, just big enough to cover the wound from a bullet, shot at close range.

Half of Dungu seemed to be Francisca's family or old friends, so it was no surprise when she introduced Harriet as "my other cousin."

Harriet was Modeste's sister, Antoinette's aunt. She wore two draped strands of tiny red beads just above the bandage, a gesture I imagined was willing life—with all its delicate frivolities—to return to normal. She was recently released from the hospital. The family had left her to heal on her own under the shade of the compound's lone remaining mango tree.

Antoinette had lived across the footpath from Harriet, and was over at Harriet's all the time, especially of late. She and her three little boys stayed longer those days to escape quarreling with her husband. He had just asked Antoinette to move out—and to take the kids with her.

That day, the attack happened in the late afternoon. One of Antoinette's boys, Herbert, was with his dad at their hut across the way. The rest hung around at Harriet's.

Screaming. Gunshots. Chaos. Everyone ran. Harriet snapped upward and saw men in camouflage with guns. A neighbor screamed *LRA!* Another: *We're dead!*

Harriet saw Antoinette's husband push chubby-cheeked four-year-old Herbert into the pathway, toward the gunmen, yelling, "Go back to Auntie's house!"

He jumped on his bike and rode to safety, leaving the dazed boy alone, in the path of the gunmen.

As she recalled the story, Harriet registered the shock on my face. In all my hundreds of interviews in Congo, I'd never before heard of a parent serving up his child to a militia.

"What can I say?" she shrugged. "He's not getting those kids."

The gunmen kicked Harriet's daughter in the stomach, knocking her to the ground. Another cocked his gun and aimed it at her daughter.

Harriet screamed and ran at the gunmen. "Oh, God! Kill me instead!"

The gunman swung his gun around, pointed squarely at Harriet's chest, and fired.

Harriet collapsed. The gunmen stomped on her daughter. Believing they were both dead, the gunmen moved on. Harriet's daughter struggled, but got up. She picked Harriet up and they dragged themselves and the children up the road. That's when they heard another gunshot and Antoinette's scream.

Someone on a bicycle stopped for Harriet. She collapsed on the bike, and woke up in the hospital.

"You're a hero," I said. "You saved your daughter's life."

She stared at me, unmoved by the accolades.

I looked at Harriet's bandage and thought of Antoinette's husband, Heritier's father. In creative-writing classes they say choices under pressure are the only true measure of character.

"I met Heritier's dad. I gave him $20 for the boy," I said.

"Well, he sure didn't use the money for that child," Harriet said.

"Where will the children live?" I asked.

"When I feel better, I'd like to have them."

By the time we reached the funeral, the family parcel was awash in harsh sunlight. Some of the men had already started drinking. A few boys stood guard as they put the finishing touches on the baby's miniature coffin, streaked with yellow wood stain; it was just dry enough for the lid to be placed on top.

Guests could have spread out; there was plenty of room, even shade for refuge at the edges of the parcel. Instead, all the women and children, perhaps thirty or more, squeezed into a shelter the size of a one-room hut, made of freshly picked palm leaves and dusty plastic tarps to block the sun. Aunties and little ones wailed around the still baby boy who rested among them on a bed, dressed in his best striped shirt and sports jacket, draped under eyelet lace, cotton balls stuffed in his nose.

Zealous explosions of color on aunties' dresses in clashing geometric, floral, and paisley patterns formed a kind of live, quilted human shroud to swaddle the departed baby, wrapping him in shockwaves of cries. Aunties and cousins sang in rounds: *Come Lord, come Lord, come and help us. Stand up Lord, stand up Lord, stand up and help us.*

Periodically the baby's mama quieted down and let herself breathe as an auntie stroked her hair. The song would wane, and then erupt again with the mama's fresh howls of grief.

Francisca and I squeezed in at the edge of the crowd, the outer limit of the shade cast by the tent, trying to not stand out, watching the uncontained anguish.

I was surprised. Maybe because back home, this kind of raw grief is saved for dark rooms with closed curtains, or because our cultural icons of strength in untimely grief feature silent tears behind black veils. Maybe.

Maybe.

But maybe my surprise stemmed from something deeper, more insidious, floating slowly by on my private sea of assumptions, the kind so many carry through the world. This baby was the first person I'd met in Congo who had died. The deaths of Congolese children certainly didn't appear to be unusual. I had heard the endless stories, unnamed babies dying the same day as their birth in the dripping, muddy bush, or a mouth stuffed with grasses by a mother desperate to choke off a child's cries that might get many others killed during militia attacks in the Kivus.

The question to Congolese mothers wasn't *Have you ever lost a child* but, rather, *How many?* So common were the deaths of Congolese children under the age of five that when I met with women in South Kivu, mothers would often wave fingers indicating how many children they had lost.

At the funeral, the unending wailing wasn't just coming from the mother. I watched a girl near the body. She was a pre-teen. I guessed that the baby was her special little friend, that she had played with him while his mama cooked and cleaned, just like the older girls did at Mama Koko's parcel.

This wailing wasn't for the sake of ritual, manufactured or dramatic, as one sometimes sees on televised mega-church broadcasts, with flailing arms and speaking in tongues. Even the stoic Mama Koko wiped away tears. Despite the caring and running and volunteer work and movement building I had done, I somehow pictured the death of a baby here—in Africa, in Congo— as landing softer because it is so common, in some unconscious equation calibrating grief in proportion to predictability of the loss. I imagined it might be less of a shock.

I was wrong. Of course I was. The death of a baby in Congo, by militias or not, arrives with the same slicing agony as it does everywhere.

I thought of motherless Heritier.

Mayano

• • • •

Our driver Mayano slipped into the funeral and whispered something to Francisca. Apparently he wanted to leave to pick up some money, promising to come back soon. By now he should have known: His availability and readiness for an emergency escape from the LRA was the whole point of hiring a car. Taking off for a few hours midday, while we were in Bamokandi, left us unprotected and exposed. Safety had to come first.

"No," I said, without further explanation.

Back at Mama Koko's, he asked Francisca again, hoping to leave with the car for a while. Francisca told him flat out "No," again. A few minutes later, Mayano walked down the driveway with a yellow bungee key chain belonging to Francisca's brother and mounted Antoine's moped.

Fear of being stranded in an LRA attack pushed me to my feet. I yelled, "No!"

The family exchanged uncomfortable looks between themselves.

Mayano dropped the subject and returned Antoine's key, but he refused lunch and sulked the remainder of the day. Noting the tension, Francisca said, "I don't like being around grumpy people." I wasn't sure if she was talking about Mayano or me.

Back at the Procure, Francisca spoke with a nun about the situation and insisted on a new driver. She reported back, "It's serious. He could lose his job."

That evening, as we sat out on our stoop eating dinner, Mayano sauntered over. As though letting us down easy, he said, "Tonight will be my final service for you."

We didn't say much in return.

"You know, they need me here," he added. "I can't take care of everyone."

When he left, Francisca commented, "He's just showing off, acting big. He thinks he quit."

But in the morning, he was there, ready to take me to a morning Internet session. He approached Francisca. "So, I need you to tell the Procure I'm the best driver here."

Francisca laughed him off. But he came back later and asked her again.

The next morning, he spotted me and forced a smile, anxiously waving hello across the courtyard. He approached Francisca, laying out the plan: "First I'll take Lisa to her Internet, then I'll come back here, pick you and your mom up, drive you to her place. I'll wait all day."

Francisca shook him off; we had already hired another driver, Mamba. I asked, "What's his deal? Why does he keep coming around?"

"They are sending him out to deliver food in LRA territory," Francisca said.

The Procure had given him his new assignment: driving the mission truck out to the Red Triangle, the epicenter of the violence.

When I saw him around the Procure, he wore his desperation like someone on death row. Strike that. Like someone I had put on death row. Francisca reminded me that the other drivers had been making the drive. All the same, driving to those villages was like a death sentence.

Heritier

. . . .

Among the resting mamas and babies, Heritier's hospital bed was empty. I circled, and found him lying on the bare floor between two rusty beds, alone, covered in crumbs. He was staring into the distance, quiet, like a child who has given up, retreating beneath his own skin.

I thought of his mother Antoinette's body, binding him in her cold arms, her breast exposed. How many hours had he wrestled, in waves of crying, waves of stillness? Why did the neighbors who found them in the morning leave him there on her body? How much time did it take for the neighbor boy to run all that way into town, to travel the mile stretch, to find Heritier's Grandpapa Modeste or his aunties? How much time to lead them back to her body and the baby, cemented to her in her stiffened arms? How could those neighbors not pick him up?

Standing over him alone on the floor, though, I paused just as they likely did: *He isn't mine. It's not my job to gather him up.*

But if he were mine, I decided, I wouldn't let him off my body. I would strap him on, snuggle him, and let my body heat radiate to warm him up from that cold night.

Who were his people, anyway? The father who would hurl his four-year-old toward a militia? His elderly auntie recovering from a gunshot wound to the chest? The miscellaneous others who would leave him alone on the floor of the hospital, covered in crumbs, resigned to stare at the ceiling?

My fingers pressed into his squishy belly. I scooped him up, grabbed the corner of my shirt, and rubbed his face clean.

He collapsed his head on my shoulder.

He appeared to need that shoulder, my shoulder. Me.

It stirred something in me I couldn't have articulated a moment earlier. I couldn't have understood it. I had mastered the art of impersonal compassion, but I considered "needing to be needed" a weakness. It was a strange new feeling for someone who has stacked her whole life toward independence, flexibility, and the pursuit of the greater good. Now, in an instant with Heritier, the choice to live alone, keeping no one terribly close, seemed like its own kind of irrelevance. The feeling was personal. The feeling was love.

His younger aunt reappeared from a bath in the back.

Francisca wanted to visit a friend elsewhere at the hospital, another cousin no doubt, and Heritier's aunt needed a break. Heritier, I decided, needed sunshine. I wanted to give it to him. I wanted to give him everything.

Heritier and I wandered outside into the sun. We sat with our legs dangled over the walkway, as we looked at the empty courtyard of dried grass. No filming, no pictures, no awake-the-world agenda, no to-dos. Just extended quiet time in my lap, in the sun. I played with his toes. I stuck butterfly and heart stickers all over his feet and arms. He fixated on a cactus-flower postcard I had in my backpack. We had a winner. He waved the postcard in the air.

His soft baby skin under my fingers mashed me up inside.

I wanted all that cold that had seeped like a virus into his bones that night, the lonely time on that hospital floor, to drain out those toes. I rubbed his little legs and poked his stomach, and decided: *Uninvited nothing. I'm going to love him back to life.*

Later, Francisca trailed behind me as I combed the shops and stalls along the main market, hoping to find a children's book, a toy, maybe a ball or a stuffed animal, a calendar with photos on it, or some children's clothes. Anything that could serve as a little love gift. There wasn't a big market for luxury items in Dungu.

Shops displayed only shiny polyester tuxedos or party dresses for children, mixed in among practical household goods. A soccer ball, maybe? But older kids would snatch it from a baby in no time.

We moved on to the open-air market, where they sold "lift and throws." I took to digging and sorting, hovered over the piles of used American clothes, as if to cover a dirty secret, searching for breathable cotton in baby-boy blue. Francisca stood behind me, amused. I pulled out some clean onesies that fit the mark. When I got to five, she said, "I think it's enough, yeah?"

There were no toys. I took a second look at scrubbies and bright plastic combs that might double for one. But on the way out, a bright green and yellow plastic rattle caught my eye, perhaps the only toy for sale in Dungu.

I tried to obscure the stacks of baby clothes and bright rattle from public view, embarrassed by the smoke signal for my newly pulsing maternal instincts.

I went to the hospital on my own and found his auntie out back, again taking a clothed bucket-bath in the common area. I knew better than to pick him up while she stood right there. Instead, I hovered and waited too long for my gifts to appear to be a casual gesture. I waited while she bathed and dressed him in one of the blue outfits, wrapped up in my newfound maternal affection.

The Red Triangle

· · · ·

Mama Koko stared me down across the smorgasbord lunch filling her dining room table. For weeks now, she had obliged the probing questions, the hours I kept Francisca out and about and away from the family. *But Bangadi?* Francisca had filled her in on our plans: a day trip to the town at the axis of the "Red Triangle," the area with a ceaseless flow of abductions, gunshot wounds, and machetes to the head. I figured we needed the most recent, most hard-hitting, hence most relevant stories in order to make the biggest difference. At least that's how I'd always done it before.

Francisca told me she wanted to go. She told me her brother was buried there and she'd never seen his grave. Paying her final respects was reason enough. Secretly, she didn't want to go. She didn't want to disappoint me, though, so she kept her reservations to herself.

Mama Koko looked me in the eye across the table. She could read me, the same way she was able to look Kevin in the eyes and sense he was for real. I knew she saw something behind my electric draw to danger, to the epicenter of atrocity.

Hers was a one-word protest. "Why?"

Francisca tried to explain about the relevance of recent stories and the visit to her brother's grave. I wasn't sure our answer—my answer, really—was good enough.

We went anyway, or at least tried to. When we got to the airport hangar the next morning, a stalky Canadian pilot squinted at the sky and told us we'd have to wait. The clouds were too low, let's see what happened by afternoon. Maybe they'd burn off.

Why?

Standing in the airport hangar watching the low cloud cover, I contemplated Mama Koko's question. In one word, she had nailed that elusive question I'd skirted for years. In some ways, I was living young Dette's escape dream. I had arranged my life to minimize attachments, eliminate dependents, and maximize flexibility. It was one thing for me, the loner, the *célibataire*, to take those risks. But Francisca—Mama Koko's daughter? The deaths of Mama Koko's loved ones weren't remote. She couldn't hide behind video monitors or black ink in a moleskin notebook, the way I had trained myself to do so many years ago.

An anxious, stout Italian priest roamed the back of the hanger and eventually introduced himself as Father Ferruccio. He was hoping for a free ride back to LRA territory. He was friendly but jumpy as we exchanged hellos and told him our destination. "Oh, no. It's not safe."

He held out his arms, revealing deep scars. "LRA."

I couldn't do it. I canceled our flight.

Kevin called later that day. He'd heard from my mom that we were planning to go to Bangadi. He rarely commented on Francisca's choices, and had never tried to persuade her to skip the original trip from Portland, even after the Bamokandi attack just before our departure. He respected her autonomy too much and had no interest in playing the role of controlling husband. But that day, he left word with her brother. *Please, don't do it.*

I let Bangadi go.

Dutch Super Wax

• • • •

That night, staring into the distance on the Procure stoop, Mama Koko said, "I don't understand why I've lost so many people."

She swam in memories of her departed. "If Justine were here, she would have been all over Lisa," she said of Francisca's younger sister. "'What do you want to eat? I'll have it on the table for you!' Just like with Kevin."

"This dress was Justine's," Francisca noted. It was one of Francisca's wardrobe regulars. Years ago on a visit, Francisca brought a new dress made of high-end Dutch Super Wax from Holland. Justine fingered the beautiful top.

"It's expensive," she said.

"You're expensive!" Francisca countered. "You want it?"

Justine burst out laughing. "I won't be shy."

Francisca didn't notice until she reached home that Justine had slipped one of her own dresses into Francisca's bag while Francisca was busy saying her good-byes.

Justine loved that Dutch Super Wax dress. It was her favorite. When she fell ill and died a few years later, she was buried in it, in Mama Koko's yard.

Francisca's brother Nico was killed for a wristwatch that Francisca had brought him as a Christmas gift from America. About ten years before our visit, her brothers Antoine, Nico, and Claude rode their bikes to Bangadi to shop. In the market, Congolese army officers spotted the fancy watch, and wanted it. They stopped Nico and demanded that he turn it over. But it was precious to Nico, as much for being from his big sister as for its functional elegance. He refused.

The soldiers pounced.

Antoine and Claude tried to pull the army officers off of Nico. But they shot Nico anyway, and beat him to finish him off, in front of the whole town. Antoine and Claude dragged his bloody, bruised body away, desperate to get him to the hospital. He died on the way.

The brothers couldn't face pulling up to Mama Koko and André's home with Nico's body slumped across the back of their bikes. Grandfather Bi's twin, Siro, had a daughter who lived in Bangadi. She allowed them to bury Nico in her yard.

When Mama Koko and André found out, there wasn't time to grieve. The war in South Sudan was boiling over, pushing masses of refugees and militia into Dungu. The family retreated to the bush, for their first stint as refugees since the Simba situation in 1964. Still aching from the loss of Nico during their retreat in the forest, Mama Koko watched André slip further away, becoming more and more ill, talking in circles about bringing children into this world to bury their parents, not the other way around.

"Dette?" André said one night. That's what he still called Mama Koko, always that young, long-haired, gap-toothed beauty in his eyes. "Can you warm some water for my bath? It will be your last job for me."

"What did you say?" she asked.

"I was just joking," he laughed.

He washed himself down, then asked Dette to bring him his best suit.

"What do you want to get all dressed up for in the middle of nowhere?" She grumbled as she dragged out the suit. "We're in the bush."

"Can you make me some tea? It will be the last thing you do for me."

"This is too much," she said. "And there's not enough sugar."

"I'll share with everyone."

Dette made the tea. André sipped, then passed the cup around. Everyone had a drink.

"Come, sit close to me," he said to Dette. She leaned against his back so he could rest against her. His breathing grew strained, then slowed.

"What's wrong?" she asked. No answer. He couldn't speak anymore through the breathing. Within minutes, André was gone.

How do you grieve in a forest? How do you pay respects? The notion of burying André in the bush enraged the whole family. Never, ever would they bury him there, they all agreed.

Papa Alexander, Mama Cecelia, and the boys accompanied Mama Koko, carrying André's body all the way back to Dungu to their parcel, which by then was swarming with Congolese soldiers.

They didn't ask permission. They told the officers, "Our father is dead. We're burying him on his own property."

The Italian Priest

. . . .

Our new driver Mamba was experienced, a serious man, only recently displaced by LRA violence up north. The Procure-assigned push-start crew, who rode along with us in the Runner's trunk space, had stayed on following Mayano's departure. Even so, the Runner was more and more reluctant to start. Growing crowds of bystanders watched us become engulfed in black fumes, often jumping in themselves to help get the old bird going. Even when our spontaneous crew swelled to six or more children and Francisca and me, our beloved Runner would lurch and die after moving ten yards, twenty yards, fifty yards before again rumbling to attention.

The irony of the Runner's nickname—appropriate because it didn't run, or because so many people had to run behind it to get it moving—earned plenty a chuckle. But on the outskirts of Bamokandi, next door to the new LRA campground, where we were headed again, it was a problem. If gunmen surfaced at the wrong time, the iffy getaway plan could cost us.

Francisca pulled our new driver Mamba aside to talk it through during his first couple of days on the job. Mamba was shocked: "You think I'm going to *drive* you out of an LRA attack?" He told her flat out, "You've never lived through it. There's no time to *think*. If the LRA comes, everybody *runs*. I'm going to *run*."

And so it goes. My rigorous safety plans were but a dream, a lark, a callow fantasy. We would have been better off with hers and hers bicycles.

Francisca did think about telling me that my safety plans were for naught, that our only LRA escape routes would be by foot, not with the Runner. But then we had people to see, stories to collect, and she had my increasingly edgy temperament to avoid. And, of course, Francisca's maternal instincts kicked in. I was about the same age as her daughters and she debated whether she would tell them about the risks or protect them from reality. She kept it to herself, hoping to insulate me from the unforgiving environs into which we had plunged ourselves.

Mama Koko watched us, nervous, as we departed. She knew. We were hoping to talk with the Italian priest we'd met at the hangar. He was living at the mission out there, near the spot we saw Antoinette's outline in the grass.

It was already mid-afternoon as we wove our way through Bamokandi's disorienting maze of streets that dwindled to footpaths.

As we drove through the entrance to the mission, ancient trees with dangling roots stretched out across the ghostly quiet mission grounds, giving the place an eerie aura. The place echoed with the soft sounds of too few remaining children. The smell of cooking smoke was much thinner here than in the rest of town. African Madonnas in the chapel blessed a parish of no one.

Father Ferruccio greeted us, equal parts warm and anxious. He led us down the mission's whitewashed main corridor. I counted twelve bedroom doors, separated by small religious icons. Only three men had remained at the mission after the recent attacks.

As we walked past the open rooms, Francisca again mentally charted our worst-case scenario escape plan, should there be an attack. *We would dive into one of those priests' bedrooms and hide under the beds. We'd stay there and pray.*

The hall opened onto a back veranda. Red vinyl chairs gave the place a worn, retro-tropical vibe. Stacks of books and paperwork lined the walls, which were decorated with maps, pamphlets, and faded pictures of priests and saints.

Father Ferruccio came to Orientale Province as a young priest in the 1970s. By way of getting-to-know-you conversation,

I asked, "Did you come to Africa because you were a priest, or did you become a priest so you could come to Africa?"

He said, "I married Africa."

Father Ferruccio settled into his chair with a cigarette and a stack of carefully typed reports about the recent LRA attacks in front of him, his eyes darting and distracted.

My ears were half-tuned to Ferruccio's desperate reports as I tried to listen, over the screeching of monster flies, for the sound of cries or a gunshot. *Did I hear screaming? Who was that?*

I looked to Francisca as a sanity check. Nothing. It was just the flies, circling my head in a halo of white noise.

With the air of someone trying to stay calm in a house fire, Ferruccio read the reports aloud. He described a baby's head smashed like peanuts in a mortar and pestle, followed by a pause to make sure that what he said had registered. A woman who was bound along with more than a hundred neighbors watched every one of them being killed, but was herself released. The gunmen told her, "It's not your time."

She was left to spread the word. This is how one hundred men can maintain nearly complete control of an area the size of California: Lone survivors could tell the story of fates so bloody and ferocious that no one will come after them. So bad that just hearing about it stings and the whole world will stay away.

Father Ferruccio was a talker. Cigarette smoke curled above him, lending grace to his staccato reports, relaying LRA massacre after massacre in graphic detail. The minutes crept toward late afternoon, into the inauspicious hours when the LRA launched attacks. We were running out of time.

Father Ferruccio began to describe the day he got his rope scars.

He was having lunch that afternoon at the Duru mission with two other priests, one visiting from Sudan, when they heard a knock on the door. It was the local nurse, rattled and repeating herself. "They're coming. They're coming. There are a lot of them."

They looked outside. About forty LRA gunmen were herding children tied together with a rope and carrying a solar panel they'd stolen from the hospital. More than eighty people total, Father Ferruccio estimated.

The priest visiting from Sudan spoke the LRA's language; he had translated for defectors before. But this time, he wanted no part of the trouble that was making its way down the road toward them. He excused himself and retreated to his bedroom, as if by shutting his door he could shut out the LRA.

The LRA came in. "How many are you?"

"Three," they said.

"Where's the other one?" the LRA asked.

"He's in bed."

They called him. The priest emerged in his socks, but refused to translate.

Ferruccio tried to hide his cell phone. They'd already taken one phone. Ferruccio said he had to go to the bathroom, hoping to make a distress call. But the LRA followed him and wouldn't let him close the door. They spotted the cell phone charger on the table. "Where's the second phone?"

He handed over the phone. One of the priests escaped through the back and hid in the bush. Ferruccio and the other priest sat, arms tied, for five hours watching the gunmen scour the mission for goods. He prayed they wouldn't find all the documentation about the LRA on the photocopy machine or on his computer—maps, photos, locations of camps, his work helping defectors only the week before. *If they find that stuff, they'll know I'm a spy against the LRA. I'm dead.*

He watched the children tied up, blistering in the afternoon sun, and thought about how their lives were over, the girls soon to be "wives," the boys soon to be soldiers.

The gunmen rolled out Ferruccio's car and set it on fire. They burned the mission to the ground and then tied Ferruccio's arms up behind his back, cranking the ropes into a bloody tourniquet before leading him down the road. Then, inexplicably, they stopped, untied him and a few other adults, left them in a hut, and continued down the road with the children.

Father Ferruccio escaped to a local church deacon's house.

"It's four." Francisca brought me out of Father Ferruccio's story and back to the reality of the day, back to the hour of our self-imposed curfew. We should have been back at the Procure by then, if not at least on our way.

I started to contemplate: Stay and continue with Father Ferruccio's story, or play it safe and pack up?

Suddenly from outside: *bam bam bam bam bam.*

I sat up straight: "What was that?"

Father Ferruccio and Francisca both smiled, reading my paranoia, and waved to reassure me. The sounds of construction hammers, from a project down the road.

I leaned back in my chair, my heart still racing, and Father Ferruccio continued his story.

Everyone in Duru scattered in the night. There was no moon. The only light came from flames glowing around Duru: More than two hundred huts, the homes of his parish, were burning into embers all across the village.

He waited at the deacon's house. Around eleven o'clock, the moon came out, casting enough light for Father Ferruccio to see his way back to the mission. Almost every building was burned to the ground. The big cross in front of the church was broken. But the chapel was intact. He found his robes on the floor. He put them on and went back to the deacon's place to sleep.

In the early morning, with the village still smoldering in the dark, Father Ferruccio emerged from hiding into the utter stillness. The LRA could have been anywhere. Alone, Father Ferruccio inched his way through the dark, back to the chapel, where he prepared for Mass.

Father Ferruccio rang the church bells.

They sounded through the ashen air, through gunmen-pregnant bush.

Parishioners crept from their hiding places, their dim or covered corners, and straggled into the chapel. About fifty people shuffled in, rough from shock, twigs and dirt mixed with crusted blood, ash smeared over Dutch-wax cloth that reminded them that only yesterday they were still human.

They stood quietly through the candlelight service, a morning Mass, a good-bye Mass, a Mass for the dead. Some wept. All took communion.

Why on earth would he ring the church bells? I wondered. Every breathing thing that night craved nothing more than a deep, dark hole to hide in and the discipline to make not a sound. That night, each villager cleaved to a singular private wish: Don't let the LRA find me.

But Father Ferruccio rang the church bells.

"Wasn't that dangerous?" I asked. "Why would you do that?"

Father Ferruccio mumbled in his Italian-French to Francisca, then turned to me and pointed his finger firmly at the sky. He said in English, "Because *victory* belongs to *God.*"

On our way out of the mission living quarters, something clicked. *Duru. Duru* . . . the family coffee plantation was in Duru. I turned to Ferruccio. "The church was in Duru, you said? Did you by chance know Francisca's cousin Roger?"

"You're Roger's cousin?" he asked Francisca, surprised.

Something tightened in him, something sunk in and closed off. Something he wasn't ready to tell us. He and Francisca spoke in a mix of Lingala and French that I couldn't follow.

Francisca explained, "Roger's wife was active in the church."

I interrupted. "He died in the attack. Did you know him?"

"I performed Roger and Marie's wedding celebration that August, in 2008," Ferruccio said. It was only a month before the attacks began.

I was surprised to hear that their wedding was so recent. Roger and Marie had lived together for around twenty years. I thought they were legally married, and had grown children.

"Was Marie a second wife or something?"

Marie was a woman of God, Father Ferruccio explained. She wanted to administer the sacrament of communion during Mass—an honor that required the priests to bless her hands, which could happen only if she had a proper church wedding. So they put on a celebration, as though Marie was still a young bride. The whole village of Duru was invited. People traveled from as far as Dungu and Sudan to attend. Roger bought a new suit and tie. Marie wore a new traditional wax-print gown. Ferruccio performed the ceremony. The party lasted two days.

Can I Take Him for a Little While?

• • • •

Some days, we went to see Aunt Harriet, bringing her a basket of food or a bottle of ibuprofen, which, she reported, didn't do much to take the edge off aching bullet wounds to the chest.

One day, as we ducked into Aunt Harriet's *yapu,* I found Heritier sitting inside, much to my delight. He was home from the hospital, sitting next to his younger auntie, who was lying on a straw mat on the floor, too ill to sit up. (Her HIV was raging, I later found out.) Heritier's two older brothers would be coming later that day to resettle with Modeste and Harriet. Their dad would not be taking them on.

I picked him up and set him on my lap. He *smiled*—a revolution since our last visit at the hospital. *Does he recognize me?* He still had the green and yellow rattle, shaking it back and forth with vigor. The plastic had broken, so the rattling ball popped out. We stuffed it back in and he went on rattling. I pulled out more butterfly and heart stickers, tickled him, and touched his hair. Every time a giant UN truck drove by, he gasped with excitement.

He fixated on grabbing my fingers, pushing them away, pulling them back, smiling. Sometimes he would reach up to my mouth and move my jaw up and down. Up and down. The night his mom had stopped moving, he must have tried for hours to move her stiffening hands, her jaw, to wake her up. Moving my hands, shaking them, moving my mouth seemed to reassure him. I was alive.

Aunt Harriet watched us play. "Take him and me with you when you go back to America!"

After a couple of hours, it felt like time to leave. I set him down next to his young aunt. He collapsed, crying. It was time to make an exit, but I picked him up again. He hushed and rested his head on my shoulder.

As he calmed, Aunt Harriet reached out to take him, and he lost it—not with the fussy protest of most babies but with a trauma-infused, desperate squeak. He dug his baby nails into my arm and buried his little head in my neck, sobbing.

"He's wasting your time," his young aunt said. After several attempts to soothe him and slip out, I had to set him down and walk away, down the street, with his howls trailing behind us.

I couldn't stop thinking about him. It was February 6, my thirty-fifth birthday. We were planning a little family party. I was to cook. On our way to the market, Francisca said, "Children sense who loves them."

The market was barren, most of the aisles sketched out but empty, so many vendors with just a few piles of beans, salt, small red onions, and a bit of garlic. Yet Dungu just happened to be well stocked with ingredients to make one of the only dishes I knew how to cook: noodles with peanut sauce.

Francisca and I roamed the market, looking through scant piles for the garlic, ginger, peanuts, and onions needed for my specialty. Someone called out to us.

It was Father Ferruccio, who pulled up to us on his motor-bike, waving us down. "I have something for you! I'll drop it by . . . ."

Back at Mama Koko's parcel, I chopped piles of onions, eyes watering, unable to stop thinking about Heritier. Hovering over bubbling peanut sauce on the brick stove stuffed with charcoal, a swarm of *what-ifs* circled. Every adopt-an-orphan thought I'd ever had was in full bloom. I dreamed of trick-or-treating and school pageants. I mapped out a daily schedule that would still allow time for me to be a writer and activist.

The peanut noodles were a big hit (soon to become a family regular, Francisca later told me). We all enjoyed orange sodas and cookies after the meal, with enough smiles to feel like much-needed fresh air. Still, something was missing.

I took some of the noodles and peanut sauce over to Aunt Harriet's. Francisca sent me with a note in Lingala: *I made it*. I offered Harriet and Heritier my peanut noodles. He loved it, which I interpreted as confirmation that I might, in secret fact, be capable of mothering. This time I got out the door and into the street before he started to cry.

The next day I had Francisca write out a request in Lingala for Heritier to come to Mama Koko's for a visit: *Can I take him for a little while? I'll bring him back.*

His sick younger auntie read the note and looked at me, sizing up the situation. She picked Heritier up, washed him, dressed him in one of his new outfits, and sent us on our way.

At Mama Koko's, sisters and cousins laughed to themselves. "Doesn't she know he doesn't have a diaper on? He'll pee all over her lap!" But we had a grand time, watching home videos on my Blackberry of my cats, and of birds in the snow. Heritier liked postcards of Mt. Hood, stickers, pineapple, and more of my peanut noodles. The payoff for the day? An uptick in his smile frequency.

I'd already bonded with Francisca's little nieces and nephews. Two-year-old Narcissis was so terrified of my white skin during our whole first week in Congo that she screamed and ran away at the sight of me. We've since become the best of friends, sharing rounds of campfire songs about making peanut butter and jelly sandwiches, translated into Lingala.

But Heritier was different. Everybody could see that. "Look around," Francisca said. "Children love you. You already have children everywhere."

One day, inside Mama Koko's, I fed Heritier his favorite supersweet pineapple at the dining table. A young mother, one of Francisca's cousins, spotted us and crouched down to him. "Is this your new Mama?"

I died inside. What the hell was I doing? I wondered if I was setting up Heritier to lose someone else.

He nodded at her, raising his eyebrows, and said one of his few words: "Yeah."

Papa Alexander: The Second Sitting

• • • •

We settled back into Mama Koko's cement living room with Papa Alexander. He seemed less anxious to talk to us than on our first day. Francisca wasn't clear why. Based on the deep and sometimes bewildering questions I had asked others ("What did it smell like that morning, after the thunderstorm?"), Francisca sensed that we might be on the verge of trampling into raw and unwelcome terrain.

Still, we picked up where we had left off.

After the family buried Roger, they split up. Mama Cecelia and Papa Alexander grabbed their nine-year-old grandson Dieu Merci ("Thank God") and slipped into the forest for cover, hoping to make their way to safety like the rest of their neighbors, either to Dungu in the south or to Sudan in the north. They walked silently through the bush.

Until they saw the LRA.

And the LRA saw them.

They ran.

The gunmen followed.

Papa Alexander was ahead, beating back bushes, until he noticed there were no footsteps behind him. He looked back. Dieu Merci and Mama Cecelia were surrounded by gunmen. They were already under orders, peeling off their clothes.

Dieu Merci stood naked while the gunmen rubbed down his small, nine-year-old body with special oils, anointing him a new boy soldier. Dieu Merci stared at Mama Cecelia, unable to stop the tears from spilling down his stony face, paralyzed with fear.

One of the gunmen noticed Dieu Merci's heavy stares at Mama Cecelia. He coached the boy, "Forget about them."

Mama Cecelia locked eyes with Dieu Merci, giving him a piercing look. She said, "You will be okay." As if willing it to be true.

Papa Alexander could have kept running. He could have escaped. But the gunmen had Mama Cecelia and Dieu Merci. All the fight drained out of him. He turned and walked straight back to them—and the militia.

As oil dripped down Dieu Merci's body and Mama Cecelia stood naked, prepped for execution, waiting, Papa Alexander walked straight up to the gunmen, with one request. "Kill me, too."

Bewildered, the gunmen said, "Old man, do you even understand what you are asking?"

"I can't live without her," Alexander said of Cecelia.

They told Papa Alexander to strip.

Once he was naked, they hit him. Kicked him. Knocked him to the ground with painful blows against his bony frame. They beat him until all the dignity he'd spent a lifetime building—wealthy farmer, patriarch, man with four wives—had drained from him and all that was left was his raw and broken body, shriveled up in pain on the forest floor.

"Get up," they commended. Papa Alexander struggled to stand beside Mama Cecelia, their bare flesh sagging with age.

The LRA cocked their guns.

One said, "Run."

Is this a hunting game? Alexander and Cecelia wondered. *Or a freak wave of empathy?* Whatever it was, they did run, as fast as their bare, elder feet could go, over sharp twigs, stones, roots, their skin naked and flopping, bruises and blood still coming on, with gunshots piercing trees and the ground, their grandson Dieu Merci left behind.

They ran until the crackling bullets faded, and they were both still alive. They ran until, in a clearing, they saw a crowd of just-released hostages. The crowd welcomed them and wrapped them in clothes.

But a lumbering, injured crowd was far too likely to attract the gunmen, so they scattered. Alexander and Cecelia limped behind until they were alone.

They never saw Dieu Merci again.

Who All Died

· · · ·

What happened to the rest of the family? I wondered.

I pictured them splitting up. I didn't think about all the things Papa Alexander had to revisit in the telling of this story, the guilt that must be eating him up: Why did they have to stay to bury Roger? Why didn't they run? How could he have left his nine-year-old grandson to people who would devour his soul? What if they had all gone together, some other way?

I asked Alexander, "So, who all died that day?"

He snapped back into the present when Francisca translated. He paused before responding. The long silence should have told us Alexander had gone as far as he could. He was teetering on the edge, across the chasm of emotions that someone who hasn't been to that hinterland couldn't possibly grasp.

"André," he said.

André was Alexander's son, named after Francisca's father.

We had already spent a long time mapping out the family tree. Alexander had already told me the names of the children and grandchildren Francisca had forgotten to note. At the time, he mentioned who had been killed by LRA, but I didn't know much more about their deaths.

"How did André die?" I asked.

"I don't know. Ask Bingo."

Bingo was a cousin, adopted by Papa Alexander about forty years before, after he was orphaned. Bingo stayed behind for Roger's burial, and he was with André when he was killed. He saw it happen. I had met him the other day, when he visited from out of town, but he had since left. We wouldn't see him again. Papa Alexander was quiet for a long while. Eventually, he said, "They chopped him up with an axe."

Francisca was reeling. She didn't know we would ask so many questions, hear so many details, go so deep, planting images in her head that she wouldn't be able to shake for years. She pictured André's last moments, and those of Roger's son Fulabako, who was with him. She wondered if they begged for their lives.

Axes. Francisca wouldn't even kill a chicken with an axe.

I asked, "Who else died?"

Francisca didn't want to translate, but she didn't want to lie. Alexander was shutting down. "You'll have to check your list." He started to crack. It was in his eyes.

I saw it. "Is he okay? We can stop."

Francisca didn't translate.

"It's okay. We'll stop."

I pretended to turn off the camera, but I let the videotape roll. I don't know why. His pain radiated, filling the room.

Trying to infuse something human back into the moment, I said, "It's so many people to lose in one day."

I waited for Francisca to pass on my sympathies.

Papa Alexander stayed transfixed on the wall, trying to hold it all back. Francisca knew better, but she translated anyway: *It's so many people to lose in one day.* Papa Alexander's face tightened and creased, as if hit by high-voltage electricity, or having taken a hard bite down on aluminum foil. He folded into a gasping sob, way beyond words or even sound.

Father Ferruccio

· · · ·

With our time in Dungu wearing on, we returned to the Bamokandi mission. We sensed there was more to Father Ferruccio's story than he originally shared. Another Italian priest greeted us. He looked like the sort of slender, aging hippie you might see at the local Portland co-op, with trimmed white hair, deep wrinkles, and tufts of fuzz like cotton balls sticking out of his ears. He sent someone to get Father Ferruccio while we waited on the mission's front porch, chatting as best we could through the language barrier.

I mentioned Kony.

"Kony," he said, swinging his arm like an axe. "Cut him down." Not what I'd typically expect from a peacenik priest, but the sentiment seemed universal in Orientale.

Father Ferruccio appeared and ushered us inside the mission, into a dim dining room with all the shades drawn. He placed fruit and coffee between us on the wooden table, an offering for our meeting. As he poured himself a cup, Ferruccio explained: The morning of the attacks an LRA defector showed up at the mission. Residents brought the defector to the church first, hoping the priests could help turn the LRA over to the UN. It hadn't gone well before. As a result of several slip-ups and UN no-shows, two, six, ten LRA returned to the bush, instead of repatriating. Two plus six plus ten LRA who would be home, doing no harm.

The morning of the attack, Roger and the area chief, Raphael, showed up at the mission along with an LRA soldier seeking asylum. But the UN and even the local authorities weren't able to oblige. If UN authorities had come, of course, they would have been on the ground just before the attacks. They could have protected villagers.

But they were busy.

Father Ferruccio asked Roger and Raphael to take the defector into Dungu. Roger had a motorbike and had taken defectors in before. The last time, only a week prior, the UN didn't even reimburse his gas money. Roger didn't want to do it again. But he understood community service, and Father Ferruccio had asked. He agreed to be the driver.

I asked if Father Ferruccio held the United Nations responsible for the deaths in his parish and village. He said without hedging or qualifiers, "Yes." If Roger hadn't agreed to deliver the LRA to the UN, he might have lived. His entire family might have made it out whole.

I wanted to say something, but any gesture—a hug, or a canned phrase like "It's not your fault"—felt too sterile.

Father Ferruccio pulled out his computer and offered to copy some of his photos onto a thumb drive for me. The computers were slow and the photos took a long time to copy. As the clock ticked beyond 5:30 p.m., Francisca and I were keenly aware that it was well past a good hour to be in the outskirts of Bamokandi.

Back at Mama Koko's parcel, the family was getting worried. The sky was already tinged with pink and orange; the sun would be going down before long. Mama Koko stood out in front of the house and stared at the road.

Back at the mission, the other Italian priest, the Father with the ear tufts, opened the front door with force, interrupting us. "Congolese army have just come back from Gilima. They're drunk."

Drunk Congolese soldiers anywhere in Congo meant trouble, from petty theft to gang rape to trigger-happy fingers, never mind those freshly returned from the Red Triangle. We grabbed our stuff and rushed onto the mission's porch. The Fathers followed us. Congolese army soldiers had parked their truck in the mission courtyard. Piles of soldiers dangled drunkenly from the truck bed.

Mamba hopped to attention and revved up the Runner. True to fussy form, the Runner sputtered to a halt. Several soldiers were already down from the truck and headed squarely toward us. Their drunk wobbling seemed to temper them to almost slow motion. Some were armed. One had a spear.

Both priests and our push-start guys got behind the Runner and pushed as Francisca and I ran alongside the SUV's open door, ready to jump in, with purses and camera bags flopping.

The Runner puttered to a halt, again. The priests and push-start crew went at it again. Again, putter putter. As the Congolese soldiers got closer, now about ten feet away, the Runner finally chug, chug, chugged to life. Francisca and I jumped in, slammed the doors, and we sped off, waving our thanks to the priests left in the dust plumes to deal with their unwelcome guests.

Mama Koko was still waiting out front in the fading light when we pulled up to her parcel.

Blood and Sunrise

• • • •

"What is this?" Mama Koko said over dinner at the Procure. She stared forward and didn't gesture behind her, but we knew what she was getting at. Serge was a sexy Congolese aid worker from Kinshasa. His room was next to mine at the Procure and he was presently chatting up a striking young nun over beers. We'd seen them around together. They were both working a mission to

deliver aid to remote areas. The other morning she came by just after breakfast in a sweatsuit rather than her nun's habit. When she passed Serge, he said, "It's dangerous to dress like that. I'm going to forget you are a sister."

Mama Koko grumbled over the chuckles and flirtation behind us in the next seating area. After a while, Serge walked the nun out to the street and the two disappeared around the corner. Twenty or so minutes later, all eyes tracked Serge as he sauntered back into the compound. Mama Koko grunted.

As daylight dropped into muted blues, the wind quickened. Lightning cracked and flashed in the distance. Beer cans and plastic bags whipped around the courtyard. Grit from piles of gravel and cement dust pelted my eyes.

All of Dungu had been waiting for the first rain. Nuns ran for cover. Mama Koko and Francisca escaped inside my room. I stayed seated outside, watching for the storm, waiting. Wild plumes of dust slammed against the motorcycles and satellite dish, scraps of garbage circled the tires on a huge orange truck carrying an oil barrel from Uganda.

But not a drop of rain. I flung open the door to find Mama Koko and Francisca covering their mouths to stop the dust storm rushing in with me. The wind slammed the door behind me.

"We're being mocked," I said.

"It's ugly," Francisca said.

"Bad omen," Mama Koko said.

I went back out into the dust storm, which was still taunting the town with only a few misty drops. The compound had cleared out completely, except for Serge, who stood up against his window, a few feet from me, as a tinny 1980s tune leaked out of a wireless radio.

A pea-sized chunk of hail hit the ground like a warning shot. Hail exploded on the courtyard, falling like screaming metallic scrapes on the roofs. Serge sang, while I looked back in through the picture-frame windows. A crack in the floral curtains framed Mama Koko and Francisca in my room sitting close to each other, lit by the florescent light.

Later, as I slipped off to sleep, a country-western song played in the distance, slowly crooning about a long road home. That night, I dreamed about gunmen.

I'm in a new ultra-modern high-rise condo with clean lines, overlooking an island in the Puget Sound. The building is deserted. The island has been evacuated, I'm alone. High-tech SWAT teams invade the island. Helicopters circle. I try to figure it through: If I could just escape the building, I could hide in the stretches of forest lining Interstate 5 to Portland. I could stay off the main roads, out of sight. I could sleep in the forest. It would take days. But the gunmen are already in the building. How do I get out? Gunshots. I have to let my people know. I have to call my people, warn them to get away . . . but who do I call? I go blank. I think to text an old lover. I fumble with my Blackberry, trying to get the message out. It won't send. There's a pounding at the door. I'm paralyzed. The men are here. I'm glassed in, fifteen floors up. The door bursts open.

I snapped awake, back into the Procure, into my slippery skin. I ran my fingers over the sheets, pilling with wear and the buildup of road-dust grime mixed with late-night sweat. Fear stormed through my veins, welled up in my chest, and spilled out in waves of sobs.

I wanted to curl up on the floor with Mama Koko and Francisca and spend the rest of the night listening to their Lingala mumblings to each other. Instead, I listened for gunshots. I listened for a knock at the door.

I cried until the sun came up.

Nonfood Items

• • • •

It had been a year and a half since the first attack, the day that Roger was killed and Papa Alexander was displaced. Alexander had not yet received any help: not a can of oil marked "USA," not a plastic bucket or a sack of cornmeal. But the long-awaited day had come on which Caritas, a Catholic international aid organization, would hand out relief goods in Dungu to those affected by the LRA. Everyone in town knew about it, and everyone in town considered themselves "LRA-affected."

The whole family set out for Father Ferruccio's Bamokandi mission in search of some help. Francisca and I stayed behind with the kids. I cooked peanut sauce and noodles again. Francisca watched the road.

A bicycle rode past, piled high with loot from the giveaway. Francisca knew the woman on the bike. She was related to one of the people organizing the distribution. Seeing those who were connected get first helpings stirred Francisca to anger. She grunted out loud.

As the day wore on, Francisca kept her eyes on the road, wondering when her family would make it home. The same first-helpings woman rode past, again, with *another* bike-load of loot. Francisca boiled. "Did you see that? She already rode by with stuff!"

On the woman's third trip past, hours had gone by and not one of Francisca's family members had made it home yet. But this woman's load of Caritas loot was piled as high as the first two. Francisca's pent-up frustration and helplessness and despair rushed into her index finger, which shot straight out, pointing at Firsts-Seconds-Thirds Lady. "Thieeeeeeeef!" she screamed, leaping to her feet and tearing up the driveway toward the street, screaming as the woman peddled faster. "Thieeeeeeeef! Thieeeeeeeef!"

By late afternoon, no one had returned.

We decided to head to the mission ourselves. We found a thick crowd surrounding the doors of a storage garage, now organized like a factory. Serge, the sexy guy from the Procure, was among the organizers of the handout day. He pulled us past the crowd, through the heavy doors to an open space filled with an assembly line of aid: the bucket lady, the soap man, Serge's nun friend handing out bright ladies' cloth.

The crowd thinned behind us. I looked back and saw that they'd closed the doors. We were to be the last people to go through that day.

Out the other end, I scanned the people who'd been shut out, who hadn't received any help. I spotted a familiar face in the crowd. There, in front of the dissipating crowd, was Paul. Bernard's neighbor, *sit sit, sleep sleep, who do you think you are,*

Superman Paul. He stayed on, as though the doors might reopen, waiting for luck that wasn't coming.

Paul was an actual, bona fide face-to-face LRA survivor, supporting twelve younger brothers and sisters. All day, folks had been riding off with bike-loads of goods, but now Paul was locked out, shut out, with not even a plastic cup.

I guess that's how it is, I thought: *Push or be pushed, grasp or sink.* The irony was that Paul was among the most LRA-affected precisely because he put his neighbors first. He volunteered to go into the fields, risking attack, after having already lost everything. He circled back to the meeting spot when he could have run, because that's how you treat neighbors. Of course he was at the back of the line, locked out without even a bar of soap to show for the day.

Francisca and I asked him, "You didn't get anything?"

He didn't.

We dragged Paul over to Serge, who seemed to be administering the giveaway.

"Bonjour!" I said, greeting Serge with an enthusiasm for him unmatched in our four weeks as next-door neighbors. "This young man survived a massacre. He has twelve younger siblings dependent on him, but he didn't get anything. Can you help him out?"

Serge took Paul by the arm and guided him to the guards. A few minutes later, Paul emerged with his own stack of goods.

That day, a year and a half after the attacks, Papa Alexander and Mama Cecelia finally collected their only consolations: a small pile of African-print fabrics, plastic cups and buckets, some bars of soap, blankets, rice seeds, a T-shirt, and a few dishes.

Witness

. . . .

Raphael was the other man with Roger on the day he died. He came by Mama Koko's to talk. We settled into Mama Koko's living room with tea, a monster-bee circling overhead.

Raphael was tall with a manly build, and he carried himself with confidence. I didn't know it at the time, but Raphael was Chief Kumbawandu's grandson. Francisca had known him since she met Roger in that elementary school. He and Roger were classmates and friends during her years there. Raphael's dad was the school principal and Francisca's boss. Their family was descended from a clan of chiefs, like royalty. So Francisca never talked to her boss, Raphael's dad, partly out of respect for their family's stature, partly to avoid drawing attention to herself. Chiefs at that time had a lot of wives—one in the area had sixty-five—and it wouldn't do for a young single woman to catch his eye. But Francisca knew Raphael.

Like his grandfather at The Bureau almost fifty years before, Raphael carried himself with the authority of a royal. He was forthright and willing to talk, but he made sure I understood that talking with me was challenging for him.

This was not the first time he had talked to a white person. Some guy from England had already been to Dungu and video-taped him. Then somebody else from America came, interviewed him, and went away, with no further news. "It's discouraging," Raphael told me. "I don't think people want to do anything. What happened to them? What are you going to do with this?"

"So let me explain what I can and can't promise. We can share your story. If Americans know what you've lived through, hopefully they'll ask the US government to do something. But I can't promise they will."

"The American government already knows what is happening here," he said.

"That's why we're here. To go back and push the US government to do more."

He showed me the machete scar on the back of his head, and began.

Raphael was the chief of the area back in Duru, just as his grandfather had been. That morning, unusually early, Roger came to his place. An LRA defector had shown up at the preacher's house next door to Roger late the previous night.

Twenty-five people had already gathered to watch over the defector by the time Raphael arrived. The crowd mumbled among themselves about the most efficient methods for execution. But Raphael told them about the law, the authorities, the Bible, and loving your enemy. The man claimed he was abducted as a boy, after all.

Raphael turned to Roger because he trusted him. Roger was a businessman, committed to developing the region. Someone who would give of himself, and not for money. Everyone shopped at his place for rice, peanuts, whatever they needed. Raphael and Roger served together on the Parent-Teacher Association at their kids' school. And, of course, Roger had a motorbike.

They knew the deal, how these things could go wrong. Raphael knew it. Roger knew it. They'd been through the exercise before: the UN taking its time, not showing up, not returning calls. The holding pattern. Roger and Raphael took the defector to the mission for the obligatory medical treatment and phone calls. Father Ferruccio called someone, who called the mayor, who called the UN unit responsible for disarmament, demobilization, and reintegration.

The mayor phoned the mission to suggest that Roger go ahead like the last time. Bring the soldier to the UN in Dungu. The UN was unavailable.

Otherwise occupied.

These were not surprises, given the time with the six defectors who were never taken in. The time with the ten defectors who were never taken in. Those would-be defectors had returned to the forest.

Father Ferruccio gave Roger twenty liters of gas. Man-of-the-law Raphael decided he'd join the escort. It was time to have a sit-down with the mayor to talk this out. Make a plan. Get the authorities to step up and deal. What were they waiting for?

Raphael, Roger, and the defector rode away from the mission.

About a mile into the drive, a pile of bushes and trees blocked the road. Roger and Raphael pulled around the bushes. A sea of dozens of killers' eyes. Gunmen. Sophisticated machine guns, rockets, hand grenades, satellite phones, a megaphone. Schoolchildren, schoolteachers, tied up with rope. Supervised by soldiers, some with dreadlocks, some with short hair, some tiny boy soldiers in UN and Congolese army uniforms. More than a hundred people, mostly LRA soldiers.

Don't let me die. Raphael heard someone yell, unsure if it was Roger, or himself. Someone screamed. It was all so sudden. Should he turn around and drive away? They'd shoot him.

The road was clogged with the crowd, so they stopped. The LRA defector jumped off the bike and scrambled into the bush. Gunmen went after him, and then turned to Roger and Raphael.

Raphael thought for a brief moment, maybe the LRA would just let Roger and Raphael ride on by? But being a chief, a responsible man, a man of the law, is perhaps the last thing you want to be mid–LRA massacre. Except, perhaps, the man who was carrying an LRA defector on the back of his bike. Roger and Raphael scanned the faces. They knew the captives in the crowd. These were friends of their children, teachers with whom they worked in the PTA. Would one of them identify Roger and Raphael? Amid the weight of heavy artillery and so much ammo, some abductees would see turning them in as an opportunity to prove themselves cooperative, useful to the LRA, and win favor.

"How far Duru?" the LRA asked in broken Lingala.

"About three kilometers," Raphael said.

The group set off in a large crowd filling the road, now surrounding Roger and Raphael. First, high-ranking soldiers passed them, then the students. For that moment, Roger and Raphael thought they would make it.

The LRA stopped a couple of kids and asked about Roger and Raphael. "Who are these guys?"

Someone said who they were.

Roger kicked his motorbike into gear, hoping to ride on.

The soldiers made hand signals to each other. They stopped Roger, and then Raphael.

They took off Raphael's boots and pounded his bike, busting it apart, and set it on fire. They threw Raphael's bike and battery in the river and bound his arms.

They told Raphael to stop on the bridge over the river, next to the village cemetery.

Raphael was not invited onward. He lingered on the bridge, tracking Roger down the road. "Why can't I go with Roger?" he asked, hoping to at least be designated a pack mule. One of them cocked his gun, as Raphael watched the LRA push Roger and another man out of the group and hike him off the trail. That's where they killed Roger with an axe. "Just chop, chop everywhere. And left him there."

Raphael watched the water, wondering if they would throw him in the river, hands bound. The gunmen told Raphael to walk into the tombstones.

"If you're going to kill me, kill me here." Raphael knelt on the bridge. They tied his arms, tight.

Whack! to the back of his head.

Out.

That is what it is like to be murdered by the LRA. Except Raphael faded back in as they dragged him, limp, through the cemetery.

Back out.

His face in dirt. Light filtering through leaves. He was in a shallow grave, palm leaves covering him, his body in screaming pain.

I'm dying, he thought.

He pushed to get up. Arms bound. Couldn't.

He struggled again. Collapsed back, limp.

He rolled over. Sat up. *Praise God.*

A jarring voice behind us pulled us back into Mama Koko's living room.

A Russian UN officer stood in the doorway with a plastic bag in his hand.

"I brought you boiled eggs. They're hard to get around here," he said. I'd met him briefly at the general store, and practiced a few words on him from my high school Russian class. But in Mama Koko's living room, as much as I tried to smile politely, his intrusion was thick under the weight of Raphael's story of betrayal by the UN.

"Oh, thanks. That's kind of you."

"Don't tell anyone, though. I'm not really supposed to do that."

We paused awkwardly. I did not offer the obvious invitation to come in, sit down, crack open some eggs together. He excused himself. "I can't stay, these people will throw rocks at my car. You need to be careful in this part of town. The Congolese army, this is really their area."

"I'm with Francisca and her family. I'm sure we'll be okay."

Turning back to Raphael, I settled back in, tape rolling. I asked again about the cemetery.

"I'm uncomfortable with the way you ask questions. Even though I answer you, you ask again. What are you going to do with all of this?"

The explanation I offered at the beginning landed weakly this time.

"Don't take it personally," he said. "But in ten months there is nothing. What makes me so angry is that everybody who used to be in my district is dead. Some people come and they put you through a process, talk about these LRA incidents, but they are just collecting. It makes me wonder if you are for real.

"Maybe one of the people coming, one person will change the world, one person will change our pain for happiness. . . . The world knows there is a problem here. Why can't they get together and finish it? People come, they just talk. They just come for the big show."

The *big show*. I wondered for a moment if that was all we could offer, to turn their annihilation into a big show, and if big shows help.

Back in the cemetery, Raphael sat up. He could walk. He found the river and managed to get off his boots, hoping to jump in and swim away, but he couldn't wrestle his arms free.

Then he heard them. The axe men were coming back. They had two men, bound, who they threw into the river to drown. *Maybe they will check for me. Maybe they'll look for me under the palm leaves. Maybe they'd kill me for real this time.*

He ran.

Barefoot, with a bloody axe wound to the head and bound arms, he wandered disoriented around the bush, hour after hour, through trees, bushes, underbrush, and finally, a familiar field. Maybe he would find someone there who could untie him? But nobody. Then he went to the next farm. Nobody. The next one, nobody. The next one, nobody. They were all gone. Hours passed, searching.

Finally, he spotted a woman. She untied him and took him to the bush, where she cleaned him up. Exhausted, he slept. In the morning he woke up thinking: *I'm going to die here*.

But then, a surge of determination: *No, I will not die running around the bush like an animal*. He found his way back to the river and got his boots. Then he went to the main road, damn it all. A mass of four or five people piled on a bike rode toward him. LRA? As they rode closer, he didn't run. *Kill me and get it over with*.

But it wasn't the axe men. It was a teacher who had been abducted and escaped. They picked him up and took him to find the motorbike battery, which had been tossed into the river. Raphael fixed the bike, hopped on, and rode.

Raphael had a second home in the village of Kiliwa, en route to Dungu.

On the road, he ran into his family searching for his body. His wife cried.

He and his wife and the children returned to their hut and settled in for the night.

Raphael hunkered down to rest, indulging his fingertips by caressing his little ones, resting his legs weary from flight, resting his aching axe-wounded head. How could he know that these precious human moments, or any action other than sleeping directly under a heavily guarded United Nations sandbag fortress, would exact a mighty price?

The knock came.

"Is that you, brother?" Raphael called.

No answer. They opened the door.

Four gunmen.

They took his children that night.

They took everything he owned and all four of his children.

He and his wife made it to Dungu, to live out a long future of dull refugee days.

One by one, months later, then months later again, the children straggled into Dungu, ointments and split skin and killings behind them.

Kuli was the last to come out, the only girl. She came in December, only a few months before our trip. She came with wounds between her legs. Her wounds didn't heal.

On January 23, Kuli died. That afternoon in Mama Koko's living room, it wasn't so long since she had passed on.

Only a few weeks between them and Kuli.

Alexander's Grandson

. . . .

I had been asking about Nyakangba since the day we arrived. He was Roger's son, abducted when he was twelve and held as a soldier for a year. Black killing powder, laced with God knows what drugs to make killing exhilarating, had been packed into split-skin crosses close to the veins on his wrists and ankles. The scars were still there. He entered Mama Koko's living room, a man-eyed fourteen-year-old.

He sat on the far side of the couch. I poured tea in a Get Well Soon mug decorated with rainbows and hearts. He set it in front of him, gentle and polite. He was cold and matter-of-fact, without occasion to hide his aching soul.

Yes, they split his skin, rubbed black powder in it. Yes, he killed. Often. (*It wasn't hard, just look at people like animals.*) And yes, he was there during the Christmas massacres, when hundreds were murdered in several villages—including Duru and Bangadi, including more of Francisca's and his own cousins. In Duru, seventy-five people were killed at a church. Nyakangba didn't say which village, but he was there when LRA gunmen found people at the church during holiday celebrations. He guarded hostages while they locked the people inside the church. He watched the LRA joke and cheer as they killed their captives. On the long hike home that Christmas Day, he took three people aside and hacked them to death with an axe, just as his father had been hacked to death only a few months before.

Only once, he saw his baby brother Dieu Merci, then turned into a soldier. He spotted him across a field.

In his off-hours, he'd think of home, mostly of his mom, Marie. Out in the bush, he fixated on her. He thought of Marie at church, of drawing water for her, of helping out around the house. He thought back to when he was still good.

Every time people were caught trying to run away, they were killed. He still thought constantly of running. When his LRA group crossed into the Central African Republic, leaving the main road and slipping into the bush, Nyakangba knew they were leaving Congo behind. They were going so far away that getting home, ever, seemed impossible. *That's it. I'll never see my mom again.*

That, he couldn't take. Marie's forgiving arms, a chance to be good again, to be helpful. That, he decided, made running worth it.

One night he was assigned evening-watch, and they took away his gun so he'd be less recognizable as a soldier. Once he was alone, he made a run for it.

He spent two nights in the bush, continuing by foot during the day, disoriented, until he heard a rooster, then someone revving a motorcycle. He knew he must be close to a home. He spotted women pumping water from a well. They stared at him. He didn't speak and neither did they. He found a mango tree, where he sat, exhausted, and slept.

Ugandan soldiers on their way to draw water found the boy sleeping under the mangoes—in a military uniform. They handcuffed him. Soon enough, he was in custody, in an office with another recent escapee, a former girl-soldier who had also been in the bush.

He answered their endless questions: Where have you been? Can you show us where their camp is? Who was there? What did they do to you?

He shared everything he knew, and in exchange for his cooperation they told him he didn't need to be afraid.

They told him to get into the back of a plane, a fighter jet with two Ugandan army pilots and a friend of his, who was another runaway LRA. "Don't be scared. We're just going to look for the LRA. Once we see them, we'll kill them."

In the air, he laughed and joked with the pilots and with his friend. They flew above the forest, scanning for the camp. Nyakangba pointed it out—and *boom!* They threw bombs into the camp and finished everybody. Then, while he was still in the plane, they threw bombs many times again, and they started fire—fire everywhere.

I saw the bombs.

I saw the fire.

I was happy.

I was happy to be in the airplane that finished those guys.

Francisca could see by the way he looked to the side, as though searching for answers, that he was lying. I had followed the bread-crumb trail in, tracking Nyakangba deep into his story. I could picture him ducking into the bush, the women drawing water at the well. I sat with him under his mango tree, resting until the Ugandans saved him with rescue handcuffs, and through the awkward reconnection with people he knew from the bush in some bureau somewhere between Sudan, Uganda, and the Central African Republic. But the giggling fighter pilots who bombed everything he wanted them to, that sounded incredible. As in not credible.

I wondered where the truth ended and his fantasy began. He seemed to want a happy ending. Happy, as in explosive revenge.

There was no tenderhearted mending under way for Nyakangba. His bone-thin, barely teenaged frame, his indifferent killer eyes, embodied everything in the family that had been destroyed. His answers grew cursory, as if to remind Francisca that she didn't know him, that she knew nothing about his time out there. As if to point to the insurmountable chasm between him and her, the chasm between him and the children crawling around Mama Koko's parcel.

After all of Nyakangba's dreaming to see his mother again, when he got to Dungu he found out: Marie had made it out of Duru. She had made it safely to Dungu. Alone, chewed up by the loss of her husband Roger and her children, after a few months, she got sick and died.

Nyakangba held on for a week or so before he snapped. After Papa Alexander's, he moved into Mama Koko's compound. Francisca's brother Antoine kept him close. He wouldn't talk much; often he didn't even respond to yes-or-no questions. If anyone tried to tease him or get him to crack a smile, he'd say, "Don't joke with me."

He'd remind them with a deadpan stare, "It's easy to kill. It's not a problem."

They hid the knives and moved sharp objects away from him when he lounged in the *yapu*. Then one day he pounced on one of the young children with a machete.

They wrestled the weapon away. No harm done. But he had to move on. He'd moved every few weeks since between extended family compounds, and was now far out of town.

What was it like to see Papa Alexander again?

I was happy.

How did you find out that your mom had died?

I'm thinking.

What are you thinking about?

Things that we did together.

What has been the best thing about being home?

Seeing people again.

And what was the hardest part?

162

Nothing.

Did you see other cousins who were out at the same camp?

I never saw them.

If you could get back into school now, would you? I'll pay your school fees.

It's too late to catch up with other kids.

Do you want to start again in 6th grade?

I don't know.

Do you play soccer?

I like cards.

Okay, cards. That we could do. But before I could grab Mamba to go to the store, Nyakangba was gone. By morning, he'd left town.

Godmothers

••••

I promised I'd bring Heritier back, and I did. After weeks of borrowing him, I felt restless when I thought of his future, recounting the facts: Heritier's mother was murdered a few weeks ago. His dad pushed his little brother *toward* the LRA and kept the $20 I gave him without spending it on Heritier's care, even when he was limp and wasting away in the hospital. Hardly a fit father.

I took to musing out loud to Francisca about adopting Heritier and his brothers, or sketching out budgets and weekly chore charts, or picturing backyard gardening projects and where the boots and finger paintings might go in my entryway.

But I had five years of life choices behind me that made the notion of adoption ludicrous. I had so de-prioritized a personal life that there was no room for one anymore. I could never pass an adoption agency's home study. I had nowhere to live. No income. No partner. Then, of course, there was my work.

Then I thought of all the Congolese women who do it, no questions asked, even when they can't feed their own kids. They just take on orphans and make it work.

Everyone could see it. When Francisca picked up on the fact that my thinking had ranged beyond the safe *what-ifs* into more serious soul-searching, she started raising red flags. *She loves this kid*, Francisca thought. *It's sweet, but it's too much*. Everybody saw him getting attached, and remarked among themselves, "That baby will suffer when Lisa leaves."

I showed up at Aunt Harriet's one day and Heritier was gone. He was staying across town with his father and brothers, Aunt Harriet told me. He'd be back with his brothers at the end of the day. So I checked back. Still no Heritier. Day after day, I stopped by to find no boys waiting, only more promises about later today or tomorrow.

Francisca was clear, sitting under the *yapu:* "The family would never let him go."

A family friend sitting on the opposite side of the lounge pavilion, a stalky Congolese-Greek man, tracked the conversation in English. He interrupted the musings: "Why not be his godmother?"

Godmother! I could do that. I could send letters and money for doctors, healthy food, and school fees.

"You aren't Catholic," Francisca said.

He interrupted her. "You don't have to be Catholic to have God. The Jewie-Jews, they have God. Everybody have God."

"You have to be Catholic to be a godparent. You are taking responsibility for the spiritual development of the child," Francisca said.

I turned to her. "*You're* Catholic. What if we were godparents together?"

"What? You want us to be lesbian godparents?" Francisca asked.

"Yes! Exactly."

We laughed, but I refused to drop it. At random intervals over the next few days, riding across town, over morning *pondu*, between interviews and visits with relatives, I peppered Francisca with questions about godparenting. How we might wire money; how I might come back to visit; how I might write letters and send Heritier and his brothers to college. How I could meld him into my world and me into his.

Several nights later at the Procure, Francisca, Mama Koko, and I took shelter in Francisca's hallway, avoiding another downpour. We spotted a young priest from the diocese across the parking lot, the light reflecting off of his slick yellow rain gear. "Hey, why don't we ask about the whole godparent thing," I suggested.

"You're serious?" Francisca asked.

"Yeah. I'm serious."

Francisca called out to him.

The clean-shaven young priest stepped inside the dark cement hallway, dripping from the rain, lit by the cool blue florescent lamp. Francisca asked about what procedures were involved and whether a two-woman godparenting team might be acceptable if one of them was a devout Catholic.

The young priest was soft and sympathetic, but clear on the church code. "Were his parents married in the church?"

No.

"What number child is he?"

Number three.

"If he was the first, or even second, of unwed parents, then maybe they could make an exception. But he was the third of a couple not married in the church. And she's not Catholic. So no. It's not possible."

So there it was. Heritier, the third so-called illegitimate child and I, the agnostic nonbaptized, were both rejects. There would be no sanctuary for us. Someone suggested, "Why do you need to be a godparent? You can always play a special role in his life."

But how? What does "special role" look like?

As the priest disappeared back into the storm with his florescent lantern, I turned to Francisca, quick-fire brainstorming: What if I just asked the family? Or Father Ferruccio? Surely he would perform the ceremony. How could he be a stickler for the standard rules of engagement in a situation like this?

I could have pressed on. I could have asked again. But I'd heard the snarky comments back home about white-savior complexes; I understood that I was trampling too far into cultural sensitivities. I was grasping at something already slipping away. It would take years to understand it. That night, the love impulse, *the take-it-on, make it my problem* drive to intervene, began to wash out in inspiration's inevitable wake: doubt.

Nights

· · · ·

Sometimes Francisca would wake up in the dead of night to Mama Koko praying the rosary. She'd listen for a while before joining in. Then they would lay there softly mumbling their prayers together.

At other times one of them would ask, "Are you awake?" They'd murmur back and forth for hours, with Francisca asking, *Whatever happened to so-and-so?* Mama Koko gave her updates: *Oh, they died. They were murdered.* Or *Oh, she's fine, just living on the other side of town.*

Mama Koko wanted to know about the grandkids in America. Francisca told her about Isaac and Solomon's indie bands, the huge party they throw every summer, so much like the harvest festival when she was a child: Everyone comes and Isaac's college friends all spend the night so no one drives home drunk. She told her about how tired her feet get from standing all day at work, then standing to cook dinner in an American kitchen.

Mama Koko asked, "Will I see Kevin before I die?"

"Kevin would come if he could, but work keeps him so busy," Francisca said.

"Well, he loves our culture. He married you," Mama Koko said. "Why can't you come together?"

"Someone has to make the house payments."

"What do you mean? You don't own your house?"

"We kind of own it. We owe the bank and make payments."

"That's so complicated."

"Life is stressful in America," Francisca tried to explain. "We live in a house, but everyone comes and goes. Sometimes we don't see each other for days."

"I think you should move home."

They began to drift.

Then Mama Koko said, "I wish the world was the way it used to be."

Papa Alexander: The Third Sitting

. . . .

Enough time had passed for Alexander to calm down from the storm of emotions stirred in our last meeting. He came around to the *yapu* and offered to continue talking with us. Together, we retreated to Mama Koko's living room.

Alexander and Cecelia had escaped the gunmen in the forest and briefly met up with the group of survivors. But soon, exhausted and injured, they fell behind the rest of the crowd. No one could hang back to help them. The more people in a group, the more twigs to break under fleeing feet, the longer the pauses when they spotted the LRA down the road, the louder the breathing when hiding in the bush with the LRA just a few feet away. Everyone scattered in hopes of a discreet exit.

Making their way through a jumble of forest and abandoned fields, grasses, palm trees, emptied-out huts, with bare feet on brush, Alexander and Cecelia struggled to ignore the stinging wounds and bruises from their beatings. Without knowing where they were going, they went.

At dusk, they came across two graves, not fresh, but familiar. In the graves were André and Alexander's mother and a young son of Dette and André who died on the farm many years earlier. The chaos of the day had spun everything far beyond the bounds of reality. It seemed impossible that they could have woven a path through the forest back to their own land after so many hours. A sudden wave of relief came over Alexander, as if he was able to retrieve his whole life, his whole family: *The attacks, the LRA, it is just a dream.*

Except it wasn't.

Alexander scanned the bush, the nearby road. *No, we are really home.* It was their coffee plantation. But it wasn't a refuge. They could hardly go back to the castle. Homes were now off-limits. Too easy to be found; too easy to turn a home into a funeral pyre. They retreated under their shallow cassava bushes for the night, though these were still too young and spare-leafed to provide real cover.

It was a one-eye-open sleep on raw dirt under the cassava, with Alexander listening for any signal to jump and run. Some days when it was clear, depending on the direction of the wind, they could hear Father Ferruccio's church bells in that spot in that field. But the wind blew in some other direction that night, or not at all. They didn't hear the bells, leaving them in the silence of morning.

"I need coffee," Alexander whispered.

"You can't go home," Cecelia said, making no move for the house key.

"I'm going. Give me the key."

They had words.

I'm not going with you. We need to go to Sudan, now.

Well, I'm going, like it or not.

Something could happen.

"Okay," Cecelia said. She threw the key at him in exasperation. "But no one is going to blame me if something happens. I tried to stop you. You don't listen."

Papa Alexander waded through the shallow cassava toward the hut, Mama Cecelia no longer visible behind him. The hut was untouched. He boiled water for coffee and scanned the stored food, making a pile of peanuts and other goods that they could carry on the days-long journey by foot. Coffee ready, he fumbled with the key to lock the hut. Gunshots cracked through the air.

That was close, very close.

He grabbed his bundle and ran back to the cassava field.

At the spot where he left Cecelia, there were only the uncertain patterns of young cassava leaves and dirt. No wife. He tried to figure it through. She wanted to go to Sudan. *Maybe she was angry, maybe she decided to just leave me, and escape on her own. The way to Sudan was the road where the execution shots were just fired. Maybe they killed her.*

The road was abandoned and splashed with fresh blood. Not drips, but gushes and pools, dragged in long trails off into the bushes. Some victims had managed to get to the bushes to bleed out alone. Blood-soaked cloth was strewn around. He lifted pieces of it with a stick to see through the blood stains, looking for the familiar ladies wax pattern of Mama Cecelia's dress. He hovered over the pools of blood, trying to intuit any clue that the blood in the pool was Cecelia's.

He scoured another road nearby and then went back to the fields. Morning into afternoon, he wandered, looking, trying to decipher if she would leave him, if she could make it to Sudan on her own, or if she was bleeding out with the rest of the unfortunate.

Alexander ground over the question *How long do I look? If she doesn't come today—no, by tomorrow—I'll go to Sudan after her. Or could she have gone to Dungu?* In the late afternoon, he thought, *I give up.* He went back home and pulled a lounge chair into the wide-open yard, and slept.

Alexander shuddered awake after a few minutes. *I can't give up. . . . I'll go again,* he thought. *The forest. I could check there.* Exhausted, he pried himself up again. Back to the bloody cloth, more blood, not hers. In the forest, he found bloody shoes that looked familiar. They looked like hers. But she left her shoes back with the LRA. . . .

The forest had been turned inside out again, and he couldn't find his way. He was lost, again.

As late afternoon faded to evening, with all options exhausted, Alexander dreaded a new round of executions at dusk and returned to the shallow cassava fields, pulled up a chair among the bushes, and again drifted to sleep, swimming in images from the last two days, and in the question of where he might go in the morning.

He opened his eyes. Slowly, across the field, Mama Cecelia waded toward him. In hushed tones, they murmured to each other.

I thought for sure you were dead.

I saw all that blood on the road.

Mama Cecelia had waited for Alexander in the cassava, until she heard the gunshots. They sounded like they'd come from their home. She thought they'd killed Alexander. She ran into the forest and found a place to burrow in. Twigs snapped behind her. Slow and gingerly she inched out of sight, hiding from whomever was walking only a few feet away. Snap, snap, closer. Sniffing and heavy breath. *Humph. Humph. Humph.* She looked behind her: A wild pig, caught in a homemade trap, paced back and forth.

As night approached, Cecelia went back to the house, and found Alexander's looping footprints all over the field.

Now, reunited, they needed a plan. Papa Alexander had no fantasies of help on the way.

It was already getting dark. They spent their second night in the field. In the early morning, when it was still dark, they gathered their things and set out for the days-long walk to Dungu.

On the main road, they saw two figures running toward them. Men, crazed and screaming: *Where are you going! Those people behind us are LRA! Run!*

The men cut into the bush. Alexander strained to see the people coming. They were still at a distance, but he could make out thirty or forty of them. He and Cecelia veered off the main road, into the bush, the grasses, the forest—far, farther—as far as they could possibly go that day.

Propped up by a tree, they tried to sleep. Alexander wanted to get an early start, but Cecelia insisted they wait. By one o'clock, they were back on the main road. As soon as they began to make their way up the road to Kpayka (pronounced "pi-ka"), they heard screaming from behind, warning them: *Three LRA! Right behind you! Run!*

There is a limit to what beaten and gashed sixty-something bodies can do. They could not hike so far off the road again. They slipped into the nearby bushes, and waited all night, again. Again, they gathered their things for an early start. But something told them to pause, to wait. Screams filled the trees and bushes. *It must be a fellow bush-sleeper nearby.* They stayed perfectly still, waiting for the gunshots, waiting for the LRA to leave.

On the way out to the road, Alexander said, "We need to see who they've killed."

They found their next-door neighbor's son, his head smashed by gunmen unwilling to spend a quick and easy bullet. Leaving a body in the forest is considered profoundly disrespectful, and Alexander loathed leaving his neighbor's son exposed in the bush. "If we had something to dig a hole with . . . ," he said.

"We can't dig a grave with our fingers," Cecelia said.

They staggered on.

It was day three with no food, as they made their way to Kpayka. Passing through ember villages, they spotted those burned alive, their ashen mouths wide open.

Kpayka was no refuge. The whole place had been burned down. They found an abandoned house. No food, but it had water and a clay pot. Like stowaways, they boiled water in the pot and took turns washing each other's wounded bodies.

It was an image that lingered with me long after Alexander's telling: the two of them giving each other a hot wash-down in a borrowed hut.

When I'd first asked Alexander what he loved about each of his wives, some distinguishing characteristic that made him pick her, he gave the checklist list only. He had married Cecelia because she was handy with needles and yarn. Francisca burst out laughing at the time, when he said he'd married Toni because she made good coffee. Alexander laughed, too, then quieted down, embarrassed. He said, "Look, I know I had the wrong thinking. But I'm with the woman I will be with for the rest of my life. That's what matters."

In that hut after days on foot, so ill, so hungry, now it was just Alexander and Cecelia—all of Alexander's wives had drifted to something else in some other town so long ago. In that moment—that swollen, stripped, worst-of-all moment—*refuge* wasn't a shelter, it wasn't a place. It was strokes of hot water on broken skin, by an old and familiar hand.

After the bath in Kpayka, they slept in the bush again.

Day four without food, day six since finding Roger's body, they spotted other stragglers, others left behind, who were crawling out of their hiding places around Kpayka. They clumped together, swelling to thirty or more adults, plus children. The others offered quiet encouragement to Alexander and Cecelia: *You're almost there. You can do it. Just walk. Just have the courage to walk.*

They walked nine hours that day. It wasn't until Kiliwa that they saw the Congolese army. When they passed, the soldiers didn't offer to help. Everyone was responsible for escaping on their own from places like Duru, Kpayka, and the villages along the way. There would be no UN, no one to greet them.

They didn't feel safe until they reached Dungu.

Months later, when Mama Koko returned from the bush and was reunited with Alexander, they sat next to each other and cried and cried and cried. Under other circumstances, she might have counseled *Give it to God,* as she so often did. Not this time. While they wept, Mama Koko could only say, "What did we do to deserve this?" All she could offer, over and again: "We're together in this. We'll stick together."

The Envelope

· · · ·

The room was warm in the late afternoon by the time we were finishing up with Papa Alexander. He relaxed as we shifted focus and retreated into questions about his life before the LRA, when life was good: the wives; the stories to the grandkids at night; harvests; his days in the cotton fields as a child; chasing off Congolese suitors who tried to call dibs on Francisca before she and Kevin married.

For a few minutes, he looked like another man. Francisca and Alexander laughed. The air was lighter. Francisca felt for a moment we had gotten through to the other side of the interviews and that the family might even be stronger for sharing the pain as they had.

Francisca's brother Antoine came in unexpectedly holding a beaten-up, reused manila envelope, and handed it to Francisca. "Father Ferruccio just dropped this off for you."

We stared at it for a moment before Francisca asked, "Should we open it?"

"Now? In front of Papa Alexander?" I responded, loathing to lose the ease and warmth we had just regained.

But curiosity got the better of us.

Why would Ferruccio drop something off to us?

Francisca untwisted the tie as Alexander watched from across the room. She slipped out two low-resolution color printouts. Each sheet had four photos patched together.

I didn't quite grasp what we were seeing: Ferruccio, with older white men in plain clothes. *Perhaps Italian priests like himself?* A young man in fatigues, holding a gun. Congolese men, civilians, standing beside the armed man, oozing dread. They looked like they'd been taken hostage. More photos, of the same Congolese men on a motorbike, with the armed man sandwiched between them.

"That is Roger," Francisca said, pointing to the driver. The other man was Raphael.

"Ah, so maybe that is the LRA surrendering," Francisca continued. "This is official, and Roger does not look . . ." *happy*, I finished her thought. He clearly didn't want to be there. He radiated fear.

Papa Alexander was watching us.

"Should we show them to Alexander?" I asked.

Francisca handed them across the table to him. She asked, "Have you ever seen these?"

Papa Alexander took the printouts and studied them. "Who got these pictures?"

Swelling with grief, he said, "It's the day he died."

"Have you ever seen these before?" I asked.

No, he hadn't; but he was already in terrain beyond words. Studying the photos taken only an hour or so before Roger was killed—the last photos of his son—had carried him into Roger's last moments.

I felt like an intruder in the room, wishing I could slip out. Every word I uttered in a language he didn't understand felt like a violation.

Alexander's tears leaked out as he went under.

Francisca had avoided looking people in the eyes when they talked about the LRA, for fear she would cry. The only way she got through interviews was to shut something off inside. Not this time. Francisca slid onto the worn foam sofa cushions, next to Alexander, and put her hand on his.

He jerked his hand away.

Papa Alexander had never done that in her life. She thought, *He blames me for stirring all this up.*

Francisca didn't get up. She sat still next to him.

Alexander got up and walked out of the room, crying. He sat out in the *yapu* long enough for everyone to see him weeping. He wouldn't talk to us again. He never told Francisca why he pulled his hand away.

Sitting alone on Mama Koko's sofa, Francisca knew that in these long afternoons and endless questions, she had broken something.

Family Day

• • • •

The last time I saw Heritier, it was the day before our departure. Francisca had asked about dedicated family time nearly every day since we'd arrived, suggesting a few weeks, which I whittled to a week, and then to the last day, *maybe*. I never felt we had done enough, collected enough. As Francisca said at some point, "You will never be happy if you are only someone who gets things done."

So that day, Mama Koko and Francisca got up early and slipped out to morning Mass. I had breakfast on my own. When they came back, I suggested Francisca take the day. She had already decided she would.

I retreated to Aunt Harriet's, my last chance to catch Heritier.

And there he was in all his soft-eyed sweetness. He brightened when he saw me. His father had finally let the boys come back to Harriet's for a visit. His older brothers came along this time: Modeste, a skinny, cheery-eyed six-year-old, and Herbert, a pudgy four-year-old with long eyes and a swollen face, bloated with pain.

Heritier snuggled up in my lap, while Herbert and little Modeste gathered around me, shy but intrigued. My-oh-my, what a serious little man Herbert was. I imagined him standing alone in the path, his father's firm hands on his back. For a split second, they must have felt like comfort, before they pushed him toward the gunmen.

I poked his belly, rubbed his head, and dotted him with stickers, fighting back images of a life where these three boys were packing their bags, too, and heading off to a whole different life we would build together. Our house would echo with storybooks and plastic dinosaurs splashing around the tub and songs Francisca would teach us from back home.

My only real-life aspiration for the day, though, was a smile from Herbert. It took hours, but finally he cracked a baby-toothed grin that barely fit between those swollen cheeks, soaked with pain and desperation, open just enough to let joy leak in.

I wanted to ask at least about being their godmother. Wouldn't the family say yes, even if the church didn't sanction our union? But I didn't have the words.

It was time to say good-bye.

I set Heritier down on the ground.

For the first time saying good-bye, he didn't cry. But as I hit the dusty road, leaving them behind, I did.

Back at Mama Koko's, cousins packed dried termites into large plastic baggies, and hunks of fish smoked over an open fire, delicacies Francisca would take back to America. Papa Alexander stopped by. Francisca and Alexander stood together on the back porch, under the climbing flower vines where so many family portraits had been taken. The left half of Francisca's hair was braided, the other half flying free, waiting its turn. They both lingered through long, awkward pauses, unsure of the damage, unsure of the remedy.

"I came by to say good-bye," he told Francisca, who avoided looking directly at him. "I'm on my way to collect termites." It was his way of letting her know he would not be coming to see her off when we left.

Mama Koko, Francisca, and I sat on the stoop together on our last Procure evening. The question of the hour hung heavy around us. *What now?*

I had already decided how I wanted all of this to end. I had brainstormed it: Francisca would emerge a leader for her country. I had no shortage of suggestions for Francisca's future leadership role, the one I had built up in my head—policy wonks to connect her with back home, campaign ideas, trips to DC to lobby Congress. They all began with one simple first step: signing up for her first e-mail account.

But after the tidal wave of gory photos and atrocious stories and family frictions, it was too much for her to even think about.

"I don't like e-mail and meetings with people I don't know," she said. "You have to let me do it my way."

The Hangar

• • • •

Mama Koko said so many times—mostly late at night, when she wasn't praying the rosary—that she was happy Francisca had come, but she would be most happy to see Francisca safely go.

When the time came, though, Mama Koko drifted away from the family gathered under the shade of the airstrip hangar's tin roof. She kept her back to us, staring instead toward a small parked plane, the one we didn't take to Bangadi.

Mama Koko was the first to hear the distant hum of our arriving plane as it emerged out of the hazy sky. Her tears fell with a wordless ache.

No one had to say it. Scanning the faces—Francisca's brothers, pregnant sisters-in-law, baby nieces munching on dried termites, nephews, the cousins with colorful wigs, the other cousins, and yet another cousin once again donning the pinstriped suit with pointy shoes—Francisca knew more would die before she saw them again. It was only a question of how many, and who.

Francisca stood close to Mama Koko. Without saying much else, they both wept as the hum of the plane grew loud and enveloped us.

The plane skipped down the dirt strip and slowed to a halt. There was no time to linger. Francisca grabbed her suitcases packed with termites and hurried through the final good-bye hugs, then stepped into the five-seater and strapped herself in behind me. She waved to Mama Koko through the airplane window.

The plane taxied and lifted off. Turning her head, Francisca looked back out the window, pressing her forehead against the glass, crying, wishing we were landing. Dungu and her family faded, smaller and smaller, and disappeared as we rose into the clouds above us, lost among endless horizons of forest and grasses.

Till Human Voices Wake Us

• • • •

Back home, Francisca got more of those late-night calls. Even years after our trip, Kony was still out there. A cousin, gone. Then another. Sometimes I'd go over to her house and we would sit together at her dining room table, quiet, while she cried.

I thought of Heritier. At my neighborhood organic-burrito shop, I watched little boys on the patio fight with each other, while eating their kiddie burritos. I imagined an alternate universe where Heritier, Herbert, and Modeste had come home with me. I would have taken them to that taqueria. I would have bought them burritos. Their rubber boots would have filled my entryway. I would have repainted my empty white walls with a kid-friendly palate—better to hide the fingerprints and show off their drawings. I would have picked their spilled cheerios up off the kitchen floor.

Instead, home felt like a swollen, empty space. No boots, no finger paintings, no cheerios.

Once, in the dry air of a cross-country flight, a statistic flashed through my head: One in three children in Congo die before the age of five. I ran the numbers, three boys, two under age five. One of them is going to die. Heritier could die. I pressed my head against the scratched plastic window so my aisle-mates wouldn't see me cry.

On an early spring day in 2012, Francisca's brother phoned her. "Are you sitting down?"

She wasn't. She stood motionless in her son's computer room. "Who is it this time?"

"Lisa's son."

Heritier.

Kony-driven food shortages meant high food prices, which meant malnutrition. Anemia took over his little body, choking off oxygen to his brain.

He had been living with his dad, who took him to the hospital far too late for B-12 shots and mega-doses of iron—if Dungu's hospital even had vitamin shots. Heritier had only a day or two before he was gone. Baby-boy fingers and smiles and soft eyes were tucked into Dungu's dark ground, like forever buried treasure.

I catalogued the *what-ifs:* Could I have wired Heritier money somehow? What if I had leaned extra-hard on people from the US who occasionally travel to the area? Could they have taken care packages—messages, picture books, flower post-cards, cash for food and medicine? Was there any way I could have brought him home? Shouldn't I at least have asked? What if I had stayed in Dungu, just to be with him? Kevin did that, after all. Francisca swore there was nothing I could have done, that even she couldn't wire money to Dungu. Even if I could have gotten money through, he was with his dad, who wouldn't have used it for Heritier. Francisca told me, time and again, it wasn't my role.

Still, I'd let go of our delicate lifeline.

And now, Heritier was gone.

For the people of Orientale, there are all the things that are gone, that will never come back.

Mayano, our first driver, drank himself to death. Heriti-er's sick younger auntie, dead. Nyakangba won't go through the programs like other returning child soldiers. He still talks about killing.

Dieu Merci has never been seen again.

Rumor has it Father Ferruccio, after all those years wedded to Africa, was sent back to Italy after a stroke.

André, Fulabako, Marie, Antoinette, Bernard, Patrick, Kuli, all gone. Roger's grave, abandoned with the plantation.

The mango trees chopped in riotous protest, gone.

Heritier, gone.

Francisca of course got more calls. One day, it was her other cousin, a nun dragged from her vehicle by LRA and burned alive on the road. "They're killing my people," she said. She stared as tears blurred her sight, then dripped onto the protective glass on her dining room table like polka dots. "I need to do something."

In 2013 Francisca went back, for her first trip on her own. Things were a little better; security had improved after US Special Forces showed up in late 2011. One morning, she slipped over to the school that she helped found all those years before, where Kevin brought her bananas and peanut butter at snack break. She dropped off some pencils. Hundreds of students were crammed into four small classrooms and a few collapsing shelters whose roofs had blown away. The children carried bricks from home to use as seats. When it rained, they all stood and held their bricks as the water ran down the walls and rushed over the floor. More than six hundred students shared only one open hole in the ground for a toilet.

Standing there, she decided that's where she'd start. Even if everything else was washed away, if only one thing was allowed to grow, she decided it had to be the minds of Dungu's children.

For all of Orientale's losses, there are still those things that do grow back. In Congo's rich soil, something always grows.

Attacks around Duru continued. Papa Alexander thought about moving back to the coffee plantation, maybe clearing the overgrown mess, cleansing the land of all those memories, and rebuilding like he did decades ago. But Cecelia said, flat out, *No.* If he went, he would have to do it on his own, because she would not step foot on that land again. Alexander won't live without Cecelia. He listens to her now. So, it was decided.

He went back to visit, though. To say good-bye, to return the plantation to the ancestors' spirits, to the snakes and wild pigs, to let the vines eat it up. Maybe one day the trees with thorns will favor the soil and thrive there again.

Papa Alexander didn't want much of anything new. Years on, he still wore the tattered outfit he'd worn every day during our visit, dirt rubbed deep into the blue flip flops, blue slacks, and blue shirt, with a baseball cap shadowing his eyes. But Francisca's brothers insisted: *It's time to live again.* They bought him a red plaid button-down with short sleeves in crisp cotton, and a sharp pair of khakis with a belt, plus new sandals and a cap—a uniform as dignified in the cafés of Washington, DC, as in the government offices in India.

Under Mama Koko's oldest mango tree, Francisca's brothers cleared the underbrush, laid a cement foundation, and began stacking adobe bricks for Mama Koko's new house. Even if she still refused to keep the good dishes, or to invest in a new tablecloth, her new home will have a tin roof, its own private sitting room, and two bedrooms, one for her and one for Francisca.

Back in Portland, when Francisca is not fundraising to rebuild the school, she dances around the living room alone. Sometimes she catches herself in the mirror, and says to herself out loud: *Hello lovely!* She spends her days off with grandkids and tends her urban pet chickens, who dart out of their enclosure to chase after her for back scratches. At work, as she organizes the olive bar, salt, or cheese display, customers might again hear her singing African hymns to no one in particular.

As for me, when I think of Congo now, I push rewind, screeching backward, past the burnt grass like snow, the smoldering cinder huts, and the smoke still rising; past Mama Cecelia's clean sweeps and washing, and the prayers sweet Marie sent floating to the heavens, hoping they'd stick.

I linger on that day in August 2008, Roger and Marie's wedding day, as though I could have accepted Francisca's invitation to visit back then because times were good, gardens were lush, and the fish were the size of children.

I imagine roaming the crowd throughout the celebration, mixing with the relatives who'd traveled all that way. I hear the Congolese church music echo out of the chapel, fading to thumping, trills, and hoots, punctuating the crowd's dancing. Father Ferruccio playing games with the children. Roger's brother André and son Fulabako, nearly men, fogging over with drink, playing it cool as they scan the crowd for girls. Dieu Merci stuffing himself on sweets. Nyakangba, the bride's go-to helper, fetching whatever she needs. Mama Cecelia's patient hand on Papa Alexander's, as the two of them preside over the festivities. Mama Koko sitting next to them sipping a beer, her wry laugh mixing with the drumbeats. Marie in her carefully chosen super-wax gown, pressed and crisp, Roger in his new suit and tie, embracing her, dancing. A time when Orientale was still the real Congo, when they were still human, still blessed, and everything, every human choice, was still possible.

Epilogue, or a Tale of Many Termites

. . . . .

Once, I asked Francisca if she thought our visit, or her families' stories, would make any difference. She said, "We have this saying: You need two termites to make oil, meaning *union equals force*. It's like if you have one termite munching on some tree branch, then another termite comes along and starts chewing, pretty soon other termites sense it. *There must be something good to chew on over there.* Then, you have all the termites chewing on the branch and before you know it, the branch comes down. I didn't think you could do it, or we could do it. But if sharing the story gets ten or twenty or a hundred more people involved, this LRA thing could be finished."

In some ways, things have gotten better in Dungu since our trip, thanks to the work of Congolese advocates like Dungu's Abbey Benoit, who has tirelessly documented human rights abuses in the region, and partner organizations like the US-based Invisible Children, The Enough Project, and Resolve. Through the advocacy of everyday citizens—students, grandparents, moms—the United States Congress passed in 2010 the

Lord's Resistance Army Disarmament and Northern Uganda Recovery Act, which mandated a regional strategy to end the violence. In late 2011, one hundred US Special Forces were deployed to central Africa to offer technical assistance to African troops hunting for Kony.

The same week Heritier died, the *Kony 2012* video went viral and more than 100 million people learned about the conflict, triggering unprecedented interest in Kony's capture and an end to the LRA. Anneke Van Woudenberg of Human Rights Watch summarized the impact of the video:

> We found so much more interest from a whole range of policymakers. I've been working in central Africa for 13 years. I've been documenting LRA atrocities since 2006 and Human Rights Watch has been doing it since the late 1990s. There have been peaks and troughs but we have never seen the kind of interest that *Kony 2012* created. It was very very exciting. . . . There's still a long way to go but the criticism of the video, which was so scathing and vitriolic . . . just completely missed the point. Kony is still out there. . . .

As of the summer of 2014, Kony is indeed still out there. People are still dying even in Duru at the hands of the LRA, which now likely consist of fewer than one hundred core fighters.

When people learn about atrocity, most often inspiration is squelched by doubts. *Who am I to help? Is it my place?* Questions like these make even die-hard activists screech to a halt.

But these days I wonder if maybe the termite chewing—all our humane efforts—is like Father Ferruccio's bells ringing through the burning night, seemingly pointless, dangerous, crazy, but perhaps a barely visible victory for God or good or love. Maybe they are like the stream-water prayers of Francisca's ancestors, sputtered out into the forest, without knowing where they would land, what forest spirit they might touch. Maybe the best we can do is release each humane act, each best effort, to be another droplet sent sputtering into the world like a prayer, without knowing what rain it might bring down, and what blood it might wash away.

What You Can Do Before Setting This Book Down

. . . . .

I recently wrote my friend Sasha—the one who said, "If you see the LRA, *you're dead.*" I asked him what readers might do one year from now, five years from now. He said, "Visit Kony in jail?"

I love that thought. We don't know how and when this madness of Kony's will end. But the damage and the structural issues in Congo's broken government that have allowed the violence to persist will take decades to heal. We can all do something to bring down that branch. Here are some top suggestions.

1. Help Francisca rebuild Dungu and Congo's future by supporting the work of Friends of Minzoto, which is partnering with the long-established Canadian Brotherhood in Dungu. For details on how you can help, visit minzoto.org.
2. Invisible Children continues to work in LRA-affected communities, including Dungu, while advocating for an end to the violence. Visit www .invisiblechildren.com, which provides "LRA Tracker" reports on attacks and abductions.

3. Check out The Enough Project's Raise Hope for Congo Campaign. Support its efforts to end impunity in the Congolese army and to fight for security-sector reform. Stay abreast of opportunities to participate in initiatives to end atrocities in Congo and elsewhere by visiting www.enoughproject.org and www.raisehopeforcongo.org.

4. Rebuild leadership capacity in Congo by supporting grassroots Congolese activists through The Eastern Congo Initiative at www.easterncongo.org.

5. Sponsor your own "sister" in Congo through Women for Women International at www.womenforwomen.org.

Appendix: Congo and Joseph Kony

. . . . .

Congo's *Heart-of-Darkness mythology* is deeply intermingled with age-old stereotypes of Africans. Few modern-day figures more perfectly fit the vision of the African "savage" than Joseph Kony: a crazed, power-hungry witch-doctor, roaming the forests with bands of armed youth, bludgeoning the innocent to serve delusional hopes of ruling a country all his own.

It's tempting to cast Kony as the bad guy because, well, *he is*. The International Criminal Court has anointed him the World's Most Wanted Man. The fact that Kony's violence has been allowed to go on—like so much of the violence in Congo—raises questions about the system in which Central Africa has broken down.

In the interest of maintaining focus on the personal story of Francisca, Mama Koko, and their family, I chose to reserve an overview of the geopolitical background—which has cultivated the ongoing system of violence in Congo—for this appendix. What follows is a very brief synopsis of a complex history, and I encourage all interested readers to deepen their understanding of Congo and Joseph Kony with further reading and study.

Joseph Kony emerged in the late 1980s as a self-proclaimed prophet and founded the Lord's Resistance Army (LRA), an off-shoot of a rebellion led by an Acholi cult figure, Alice Auma. The LRA emerged as factions fought for control of Uganda, where the Acholi people in Northern Uganda had long been targets of mass atrocities. Kony, who had trained as a traditional healer as a young man, fused traditional Acholi beliefs and practices with bits of Christianity and set his sights on taking over Uganda. His goal was to rule over the country with the Bible's Ten Commandments.

Kony did not have much success recruiting ideologically driven rebels to his cause, so he filled his fighting force with abducted children. The militia launched horrific attacks on civilians and forced their abductees to become sexual slaves or to perform mutilations, massacres, and rapes and abduct more children. Conservative estimates indicate that during the LRA's twenty years in Uganda, more than 20,000 children were abducted and nearly 2 million people were displaced.

Though Kony branded himself as a cult leader and played the part to full dramatic effect by speaking in tongues, wearing wigs, and claiming spirit possessions, the vast majority of LRA fighters didn't remain in his militia out of ideology or loyalty to Kony, but because they were afraid they'd be killed for trying to escape.

In the late 1990s, the government of Uganda forced Acholi communities into camps termed "protected villages," which were much like Japanese internment camps in the United States during World War II—possibly to eliminate the threat of their collaboration with the LRA. The conditions in the camps were dire and there was little access to food, medicine, or basic livelihoods. Because of this, many human rights advocates also considered Ugandan president Yoweri Museveni a perpetrator of mass human rights abuses.

Meanwhile, the government of Sudan—longtime foes of Uganda—provided ongoing support to the LRA in the form of military training, weapons, and a safe place to regroup.

In 2005, the International Criminal Court issued indictments against Joseph Kony and several of his top commanders. The same year, a mass offensive by Ugandan troops finally pushed Kony to abandon his camps in Northern Uganda. More than 95 percent of the people residing in "protected villages" returned home. The region finally began to stabilize; since then, donor governments have poured hundreds of millions of dollars into rebuilding the area.

But the LRA didn't disappear; they just moved next door, into Congo's Garamba National Park, and then to the swaths of forest stretching from Orientale Province in the Democratic Republic of Congo into Sudan and the Central African Republic.

In early 2006, the United Nations sent Guatemalan Special Forces into the Garamba National Park, which was serving as a quasi-headquarters for the LRA. But the mission backfired and a four-hour shoot-out with the LRA left eight Guatemalan Special Forces dead. This bungled mission not only sparked intense debates within the UN, it also scared off other governments that may otherwise have sent troops to battle the LRA. So the LRA was left, uncontained.

In September 2008, the LRA launched mass attacks on civilians in Congo. The attacks intensified by December 2008 in what is now known as the Christmas massacres. Hundreds of people were murdered during the holiday season.

During the next two years, many LRA groups splintered, sometimes operating hundreds of miles from the next group, some maintaining little or no contact with Kony, who was hiding somewhere in the bush, ruling by satellite phone. Some members defected. By January 2010, when Francisca and I went to Dungu, official estimates indicated that LRA ranks had dwindled to no more than 150 to 200 core fighters. Some estimated their numbers as fewer than 100. Nevertheless, the LRA's reputation and the terror they instilled in the people of Congo were enough to allow them to reign over the region. Even as their attacks began to yield fewer victims, locals often fled, and more than 465,000 people in Congo, the Central African Republic, and Sudan were displaced.

By 2010, in Congo alone, the LRA had killed more than 1,900 people, abducted more than 2,600, and displaced more than 347,000.

But it wasn't just the LRA and the UN's failure to intervene that led to the violence suffered by families like Mama Koko's. Congo's essentially nonfunctioning government also fostered an environment in which locals were vulnerable to attacks and distrusting of their own leaders and army.

To understand this collapse of local government—which allowed the LRA violence to spiral—we must look further back to the nineteenth century, when King Leopold of Belgium took control of Congo, making it the only colony in the world owned by one private individual. During his brutal rule, Congolese were chained up, mutilated, and beheaded by European administrators. It was during this period that Joseph Conrad penned *Heart of Darkness*. Though many considered the novel's imagery—such as severed body parts strewn around an administrator's garden—to be metaphorical, in fact, reviews of historical records indicate that some administrators did in fact keep severed heads of "natives" in their yards. Under King Leopold's rule, Congo's population plummeted by 10 million over a period of three decades. King Leopold built himself elaborate palaces out of funds from Congo's looted goods such as rubber, all the while masquerading as a charitable leader who offered the Congolese people an opportunity to become civilized and protection from Arab slave traders.

In 1911, Belgium took ownership of Congo and maintained colonial rule for the next fifty years. While Belgium focused on building infrastructure and extracting resources from the Congo, Congolese rarely advanced to managerial roles. When the Congolese people gained their independence in 1960, only nineteen Congolese people held college degrees and fewer than fourteen thousand were enrolled in secondary school. In a 1961 news report, journalist John A. Kennedy cited a conversation with a senior United Nations education consultant who said that Belgians chose to discourage Congolese from attending college because "students who were sent to England, France, or the United States to study came back as 'partially educated radicals.'"[1]

Kennedy continued, "I got about the same answers in our tour of the Congo, talking with its experts, inspecting its schools and colleges two years ago. They claimed to have profited from the mistakes of other nations who sent students from the colonies to study abroad, where they were exposed to political ideas they were not sufficiently educated to be able to criticize."

In 1960, Congo won independence and held its first free elections. Patrice Lumumba, one of the leaders of the independence movement, was elected Congo's first prime minister. He was a popular figure, a voice for Congolese ownership, responsibility, and power. He decried colonial rule and envisioned a future for Congo on its own terms. "The future of Congo is beautiful . . . without dignity there is no liberty, without justice there is no dignity, and without independence there are no free men. . . . History will one day have its say, but it will not be the history that Brussels, Paris, Washington, or the United Nations will teach, but that which they will teach in the countries emancipated from colonialism and its puppets."[2]

In 1961, Lumumba was assassinated. The United States' CIA was widely considered to be behind the killing,[3] which apparently was based on concerns about budding alliances that Lumumba was forming with the Soviet Union. A 2013 article in *The Guardian* covered alleged deathbed revelations by the MI6 operative Daphne Park:

> In a letter to the *London Review of Books*, Lord Lea said the admission was made while he was having a cup of tea with Daphne Park, who had been consul and first secretary from 1959 to 1961 in Leopoldville, as the capital of Belgian Congo was known before it was later renamed as Kinshasa following independence.

He wrote: "I mentioned the uproar surrounding Lumumba's abduction and murder, and recalled the theory that MI6 might have had something to do with it. 'We did,' she replied. 'I organised it.'"

". . . We went on to discuss her contention that Lumumba would have handed over the whole lot to the Russians: the high-value Katangese uranium deposits as well as the diamonds and other important minerals largely located in the secessionist eastern state of Katanga," added Lea.[4]

With the backing of the US government, Mobutu Sese Seko was installed as the country's new leader, and he received sustained support from the United States. Mobutu proved to be the quintessential corrupt African dictator, siphoning off approximately $5 billion into his personal coffers and pandering to Western interests.[5]

The catalyst for the present-day Congo crisis began with the 1994 Rwandan genocide. Though historically there had been little conflict between Tutsis and Hutus in Rwanda and intermarriage between the two groups was common, colonists exploited loose tribal affiliations, issued ethnic identity cards, and stoked animosity and the myth of Tutsis as a minority ruling class. Tensions boiled over at various points in the twentieth century, sending ethnic Tutsis fleeing for safety into Congo, where they established communities. Congolese-Tutsis, known as *Banyamulenge*, were never fully integrated into Congolese society.

Those ethnic tensions originally orchestrated by colonists ultimately exploded into the Rwandan genocide in 1994. Hutu militias killed at will for four months, resulting in the deaths of between 500,000 and 1,000,000 people.

A Tutsi-led defense force ultimately retook and secured the country. In the process, 100,000 to 200,000 Hutu *genocidaires*, known in Congo and Rwanda as *Interahamwe* ("those who kill together"), were pushed across the border into neighboring Congo, along with 1 million to 2 million Hutu refugees. The *Interahamwe* melded into refugee camps and organized with the aim of retaking Rwanda.

Rwanda's new Tutsi-led government viewed these forces as an extreme security threat, which they appealed to the international community to address. Peaceful options were proposed by various authorities, such as spending a few hundred million dollars on moving the refugee camps far from Rwanda's border so they no longer posed an imminent threat, but the international donor community rejected this arrangement.

With the support of the United States, Rwanda groomed Congolese Laurent Kabila to lead Rwandan forces into Congo. Kabila invaded and wiped out the camps overnight. Some Hutu civilians returned to Rwanda; others fled more than a thousand miles into Congo. The latter were pursued by the Rwandan forces, who carried out several massacres of Hutu civilians—attacks that a United Nations report labeled genocide (though the UN later retracted that classification at the protest of the Rwandan government). Laurent Kabila made it all the way to Kinshasa and overthrew Mobutu. Meanwhile, *Interahamwe* retreated into Congo's forests, where they set up camps, rebranded themselves the Forces for the Democratic Liberation of Rwanda (FDLR), and have been terrorizing Congolese civilians ever since.

Other militias were formed to fight the FDLR, then each other; several other nations jumped into the fray, and the conflict erupted into what has been termed "Africa's World War." The United Nations and many policy analysts have accused all parties involved in the war of using the conflict as a cover for looting.[6] The Democratic Republic of the Congo is among the most resource-rich countries on the planet, with more than 1,100 minerals, including tin, tantalum, tungsten, and gold. These minerals are often extracted illegally and traded illicitly by nearly all armed groups, including the Congolese army. The minerals are smuggled out, often through Rwanda, and, until 2014, ultimately ended up in 100 percent of consumer electronics products, among many other consumer goods.

In 2001, Laurent Kabila was assassinated and his son, Joseph Kabila, took his place as president of Congo. Warlords eventually engaged in a peace process, agreeing to a unique power-sharing agreement wherein the junior Kabila could maintain his presidency while heads of various factions took on the roles of vice presidents. Fighting continued in Eastern Congo, mostly by ragtag militias, including the notorious FDLR.

The Congolese army integrated several militias into its ranks over the years. But the army often doesn't pay its soldiers. Instead the army leaders give the soldiers guns and send them off to their outposts, assuming that the soldiers will take what they want and need from the same locals they are supposed to protect.

These soldiers are major perpetrators of rape. A culture of impunity and lawlessness has taken over Eastern Congo, leading to mass displacement, atrocities, and the worst rape pandemic on earth. While for the most part people are no longer massacred by the hundreds, smaller-scale violence has continued unabated and the rape pandemic has spiked.

The ongoing crisis in Congo has proved more deadly than any conflict since World War II. A 2007 mortality study by the International Rescue Committee placed the death toll at 5.4 million, with new deaths occurring at a rate of 45,000 per month.[7] According to a 2011 study published in the *American Journal of Public Health*, in one year alone more than 400,000 women and girls were raped.[8]

In 2006, with heavy international support and monitoring, Congo held its first democratic elections in more than forty years. Joseph Kabila won the presidency but his popularity waned in the following years. In 2011, the second round of democratic elections was held, with far less international technical and financial support. Though Kabila was declared the victor, the elections were widely regarded as fraudulent. Nonetheless, the outcome was accepted by the international community, which sent a powerful message that Kabila is not accountable to the Congolese people, thus bypassing an essential path to Congolese ownership of their country's future.

When Joseph Kony is captured, the damage done to the community affected by his attacks will take years to undo. Meanwhile, Congo has collapsed. The dysfunctional army, police, and justice systems, along with corrupt, self-interested government, have left regular Congolese families like Mama Koko's wide open to mass atrocity.

List of Characters

. . . . .

Alexander, also known as Papa Alexander: Francisca's uncle, André's only full brother, and the last of forty-three children of Gamé

André: Francisca's father and elder brother to Papa Alexander

André (Jr.): Alexander's son

Antoine: Francisca's younger brother

Antoinette: Francisca's cousin, who was murdered during the LRA attack in Dungu in 2010, just prior to our arrival

Bernard: Francisca's cousin

Bi: Mama Koko's father

Bingo: Francisca's cousin, adopted by Papa Alexander after being orphaned

Biroyo: Cisca's classmate

Bondo: Bi's father

Cecile: Francisca's Congolese friend in Wyoming

Claude: Francisca's younger brother

Dieu Merci: Roger and Marie's youngest son, Papa
    Alexander's grandson

Father Ferruccio: Italian priest, in Congo since the 1970s

Francisca, also known as Cisca as a child: Mama Koko's
    daughter

Fulabako: Roger's son

Gamé: Father of André and Alexander

Gamé (Jr.): Francisca's younger brother

Harriet: Sister to Modeste, aunt to Antoinette, great-aunt
    to Heritier

Herbert: Heritier's four-year-old brother

Heritier: Antoinette's baby boy, found after the attack that
    killed her

Isaac: Francisca and Kevin's first son, born in Dungu

Jean: Francisca's firstborn son, from a previous relationship

Justine: Francisca's younger sister

Kevin: Francisca's American husband, a former Peace
    Corps volunteer

Kuli: Raphael's daughter

Kumbawandu: Chief of the area in the 1960s, in Duru

Lomingo: Francisca's daughter from a previous relationship

Mama Cecelia, also known as Cecelia: Papa Alexander's
    fourth wife

Mama Koko, also known as Bernadette or Dette:
    Francisca's mother

Mamba: Our second driver

Marie: Roger's wife

Mayano: Our first driver

Modeste: Francisca's cousin and Antoinette's father

Modeste (Jr.): Heritier's brother

Nahilite: Bi's mother

Narcissis: Francisca's niece

Neseti: Papa Alexander's former girlfriend and mother to Roger

Nico: Francisca's Greek playmate

Nico: Francisca's brother

Nyakangba: Son of Roger and Marie, grandson of Papa Alexander

Patience: Francisca's daughter from a previous relationship

Patrick: Neighbor of Bernard

Paul: Neighbor of Bernard, present at his death

Raphael: Roger's friend and classmate, and Chief Kumbawandu's grandson

Roger: Alexander's firstborn son

Sako: Papa Alexander's former girlfriend

Sasha: Congo and LRA expert, friend of the author

Serge: Aid worker from Kinshasa, neighbor of Lisa and Francisca at the Procure

Solomon: Francisca and Kevin's youngest son, born in Dungu

Toni, Ngalagba, and **Monokoko:** Alexander's first three wives

Vivica, later known as Tita Vica: Mama Koko's mother, Francisca's grandmother

Author's Note

. . . . .

Mama Koko and the Hundred Gunmen is a true story. It weaves together my 2010 trip to Dungu, firsthand accounts of the impact of Joseph Kony's Lord's Resistance Army on Francisca Thelin's friends and neighbors, and Francisca's family history stretching back to the 1950s and earlier. The material is based on my memory and on notes from my trip to Dungu, as well as on videotaped and transcribed interviews. In some instances, information that was relayed to me over the course of several conversations has been compressed into one conversation. Some portions are not presented in chronological order. There are no composite characters. The material has been confirmed by Francisca and other family members present. The re-creation of Francisca's childhood and events taking place prior to our visit was based on and verified by Francisca and other members of her family.

Lisa J. Shannon
June 2014

Notes

• • • • •

Notes to Appendix

1. John A. Kennedy, "Prime Need Is Education; Only 19 Native Congolese College Graduates There," *Times Daily*, April 28, 1961, p. 5, http://news.google.com/newspapers?nid=1842&dat=19610428&id=9Jct AAAAIBAJ&sjid=zMYEAAAAIBAJ&pg=1227,6181859.

2. David Renton, David Seddon, and Leo Zeilig, *The Congo: Plunder and Resistance* (Zed Books, 2007), p. 99.

3. "Patrice Lumumba: The Most Important Assassination of the 20th Century," http://www.theguardian.com/global-development /poverty-matters/2011/jan/17/patrice-lumumba-50th-anniversary -assassination.

4. "MI6 'Arranged Cold War Killing' of Congo Prime Minister," http://www.theguardian.com/world/2013/apr/02/mi6-patrice -lumumba-assassination.

5. Lisa Shannon, *A Thousand Sisters* (Seal Press, 2010).

6. Enough Project Team with the Grassroots Reconciliation Group, "A Comprehensive Approach to Congo's Conflict Minerals," strategic paper, The Enough Project, April 24, 2009.

7. "Congo Crisis," http://www.rescue.org/special-reports/congo -forgotten-crisis.

8. Amber Peterman, Tia Palermo, and Caryn Bredenkamp, "Estimates and Determinants of Sexual Violence Against Women in the Democratic Republic of Congo," *American Journal of Public Health* 101, no. 6 (June 2011): 1060–1067.

Acknowledgments

· · · · ·

When I asked Francisca who we should thank, she said, "The little people always get left out. Let's thank Mayano. I miss him." So, to begin, the last first: a special thanks to our drivers, Mayano and Mamba. Also, to the many people who push-started the Runner in times of humor and times of drunken Congolese army pursuit.

This book only came to be because of Francisca Thelin, along with Mama Koko, Papa Alexander, and everyone we interviewed. My deepest gratitude to them for their extensive time and willingness to embark on that sometimes painful journey into the past. They did it as a service to help their homeland heal and prosper, and to show us all the beauty of the real Congo.

Specifically, thanks to Aunt Harriet, Modeste, Raphael, Nyakangba, Paul, Antoinette's brother, Father Ferruccio and the other mission priests, and Kevin.

Thanks to Francisca and Kevin's family: Jean, Patience, Lomingo, Solomon, Isaac, Mimi, Safina, and Olivia.

This book would not be in your hands were it not for Emily Lavelle, the biggest champion of *Mama Koko and the Hundred*

Gunmen; thanks to Emily's keen editing instincts and dogged commitment, the book is now the very best version of itself. Thanks also to Lisa Kaufman for her behind-the-scenes support and commitment to getting stories like this one into the world. And of course to everyone at PublicAffairs, from the design team to the sales agents.

As ever, there aren't enough words to thank the one and only Ann Shannon, my mom and go-to partner-in-crime for all things Africa, activism, and editing.

Thanks to my sister Julie Shannon, for serving as my "ideal reader" and reviewing multiple drafts, as well as my niece Aria Shannon, for reading early drafts and being generally awesome.

To Andrew Shakman, my sanctuary and best friend, for his undying support and remarkable story notes.

To dearest friend and editor extraordinaire Michelle Hamilton, as well as coach, producer, and protector Rachel Hanfling.

To Jerry Jones and the So-Hum Foundation, for early, ongoing, and always generous support.

To my agent Jill Marsal, for her early belief in me and the importance of these stories, for her ongoing support and stellar story notes.

To my dear friends Shelley Jacobsen, Kristen Leppert, Jesse Emerson, Gwen, Tammy and Amit Singh, Richa and Anil Sehgal and their family for tireless volunteer support, and Lana Veenker for her encouragement at many steps along the way.

For their encouragement, structure, and invaluable feedback in moving this project from notes to proposal to book, tremendous thanks to Harvard writing guru Jeffrey Seglin as well as Greg Harris, Harvard writing instructor extraordinaire.

Thanks to Charlie Clements of the Carr Center for Human Rights, mentor and fierce advocate for amplifying grassroots voices, and Vidya Sri, for their endless patience and support during my absence from campaign work and fellowship duties to complete the book. Also to Frank Hartmann, whose mentorship and game plans have kept me on track and implementing effectively.

Huge thanks to some of my favorite advocates working on the LRA and experts Sasha Lezhnev, Michael Poffenberger, Lisa Dougan, John Prendergast, Jason Russell, and all the non-elites who ever worked to stop Kony or bring stability to Congo.

Thanks to the many veteran aid-worker friends and colleagues who have indulged me with hours of conversation on the dynamics of international aid and the complexities of working for change in Africa.

And to everyone, anywhere, who steps up in his or her own way in the name of good, who sticks with it despite complications and criticism, often with nothing more than blind faith that in the face of atrocity, doing something—anything—is imperative.

Lisa J. Shannon is a human rights activist, writer, and speaker. She is the founder of Run for Congo Women, which raises awareness of the forgotten crisis in Congo, and the author of the award-winning book A *Thousand Sisters*. She has appeared on *The Oprah Winfrey Show* and NPR's *Morning Edition* and has been featured in the *New York Times*, the *New York Times Magazine*, and *The Economist*. In 2010, she was named one of O magazine's 100 Most Influential Women on the Planet. She lives in Portland, Oregon.

PublicAffairs is a publishing house founded in 1997. It is a tribute to the standards, values, and flair of three persons who have served as mentors to countless reporters, writers, editors, and book people of all kinds, including me.

I. F. STONE, proprietor of *I. F. Stone's Weekly*, combined a commitment to the First Amendment with entrepreneurial zeal and reporting skill and became one of the great independent journalists in American history. At the age of eighty, Izzy published *The Trial of Socrates*, which was a national bestseller. He wrote the book after he taught himself ancient Greek.

BENJAMIN C. BRADLEE was for nearly thirty years the charismatic editorial leader of *The Washington Post*. It was Ben who gave the *Post* the range and courage to pursue such historic issues as Watergate. He supported his reporters with a tenacity that made them fearless and it is no accident that so many became authors of influential, best-selling books.

ROBERT L. BERNSTEIN, the chief executive of Random House for more than a quarter century, guided one of the nation's premier publishing houses. Bob was personally responsible for many books of political dissent and argument that challenged tyranny around the globe. He is also the founder and longtime chair of Human Rights Watch, one of the most respected human rights organizations in the world.

·   ·   ·

For fifty years, the banner of Public Affairs Press was carried by its owner Morris B. Schnapper, who published Gandhi, Nasser, Toynbee, Truman, and about 1,500 other authors. In 1983, Schnapper was described by *The Washington Post* as "a redoubtable gadfly." His legacy will endure in the books to come.

Peter Osnos, *Founder and Editor-at-Large*